BASIC FINANCIAL LITERACY

D1522690

BASIC
FINANCIAL
LITERACY

What You Didn't Learn in School

MICHAEL GARRISON
TANYA BROCKETT

Hallagen Ink Press
CHARLOTTESVILLE, VA USA

Copyright © 2024, Michael Garrison and Tanya Brockett

All rights reserved. No part of this publication may be reproduced, distributed or transmitted in any form or by any means, including photocopying, recording, or other electronic or mechanical methods, without the prior written permission of the publisher, except in the case of brief quotations embodied in critical reviews and certain other noncommercial uses permitted by copyright law. For permission requests, write to the publisher, subject "Permissions," at Admin@HallagenInk.com.

Cover design, editing, and book design: Hallagen Ink

Disclaimer: This publication is designed to provide accurate and authoritative information about the subject matter covered. It is sold with the understanding that the authors and publisher are not engaged in rendering legal, intellectual property, accounting, financial, medical, psychological, or other professional advice. The authors are simply entrepreneurs sharing insights based on their experiences and education. If legal advice or other professional assistance is required, the services of a competent professional should be sought. The authors and publisher, individually or corporately, do not accept any responsibility for any liabilities resulting from the actions of any parties involved.

ORDERING INFORMATION
Quantity sales: Special discounts may be available on large quantity purchases by corporations, associations, book clubs, universities, and others. For details, contact "Special Sales" at the email above.

Basic Financial Literacy/Garrison, Brockett.—1st ed.

If you let your learning lead to knowledge,
you become a fool.
If you let your learning lead to action,
you become wealthy.

—TONY ROBBINS

Contents

Preface...*ix*

1. Opening Your Mind to What You Want 1

2. Your Guide to SMART Financial Goals 11

3. Budgeting and Expense Management.............. 17

4. Making Regular Saving a Priority...................... 22

5. Distinct Approaches to Wealth 29

6. Understanding Credit: Like It or Not................ 35

7. The Strategic Edge: Debt in Wealth Building.. 50

8. Embracing Lifelong Financial Learning........... 57

9. Retirement Planning Simplified 61

10. Demystifying Tax Planning 70

11. Insurance Planning 80

12. Estate Planning 86

13. Navigating Risk 92

14. Long-Term Perspective... 98

15. Professional Guidance...103

16. Regular Review 109

17. Staying Disciplined...114

18. Embarking on a Lifelong Journey......................120

Suggested Readings..124

About the Authors...127

PREFACE

IN TODAY'S WORLD, where our everyday lives are heavily influenced by financial decisions, not having a formal education in money management can leave many of us feeling lost and uncertain. The truth is that the lessons we learned in school rarely covered the details of budgeting, investing, or planning for retirement. Yet, these are the very skills that are essential for our financial well-being and future security.

Basic Financial Literacy: What You Didn't Learn in School is perfect for those striving to understand the often confusing topic of personal finance. This book is written with a deep understanding of the challenges faced by newbie investors, serving as a compass to help readers gain a clearer understanding of financial management principles.

In this book, you'll find more than just a bunch of boring financial facts and figures. It's a roadmap that empowers you through knowledge. Each chapter is designed to equip you with the knowledge you need to take control of your financial future, from setting achievable goals to making informed decisions that leave a lasting impact. It covers the concepts you need to understand and then provides an example of how they can be implemented.

This book doesn't rely on complicated jargon or theoretical concepts. Instead, it draws from real-life examples and practical strategies to provide a comprehensive overview of essential financial concepts. Whether you're learning how to create a simple budget, save consistently, or make wise investments, each topic is presented in a clear and accessible manner.

Basic Financial Literacy is more than just a manual for managing money. It's a call to action, reminding us that financial freedom is within our reach if we're willing to invest in our own education. By embracing the principles outlined in this book, you will not only gain a deeper understanding of your finances but also lay the foundation for a lifetime of prosperity and success.

To continue your financial education journey, we've compiled a list of suggested readings and resources to help you further expand your knowledge and skills in personal finance. Whether you're interested in investing, budgeting, or retirement planning, these resources will provide valuable insights and guidance on your path to financial success.

In a society where financial literacy is not prioritized before adulthood, *Basic Financial Literacy: What You Didn't Learn in School* provides guidance and fills the gaps between what we are taught and what we need to know to be financially successful. It offers readers the knowledge and confidence they need to understand modern finance and build a brighter future for themselves and their loved ones.

[1]

OPENING YOUR MIND TO WHAT YOU WANT

MONEY IS A MIND GAME. A mindset primed for growth and abundance recognizes there are infinite possibilities in life. This mentality, often referred to as a growth mindset, enables individuals to expand their horizons and overcome self-imposed limitations, thus fostering a conducive environment for financial success. If you say you want to achieve a specific financial goal, but deep inside, you believe that it is not possible given your upbringing or surroundings, then you will rise (or fall) to the level of your belief. Thus, if your beliefs about money and finance are not in alignment with where you want to go financially, a mindset shift is in order.

EXPANDING YOUR FINANCIAL EQ

Emotional intelligence concerning money, or financial EQ, is a cornerstone of our financial well-being, influencing every aspect of our financial lives. Our thoughts and feelings about money have a profound impact on our financial outcomes. Ken Honda, the Zen Millionaire who impacts millions with his books and presentations, shares that money is energy, and when we pay a bill or invest with negative thoughts or emotions, we carry "that energy through most situations." But when we spend or give money with happiness, joy, or gratitude, it is smiling or happy money. Receiving and spending money with gratitude brings you more positive experiences with money and improves your money relationship.

Our attitudes, beliefs, and behaviors towards money serve as the lens through which we perceive and interact with the financial world. If we harbor fears and limiting beliefs about our ability to grow our finances or achieve our goals, those beliefs will inevitably dictate our financial outcomes. Conversely, if we cultivate beliefs of abundance and confidence in our ability to achieve financial success, our actions will reflect these beliefs, leading to positive results. Many of these beliefs were ingrained in us at a young age. It takes changing your paradigm and shifting your mindset about money to start creating positive financial results.

Cultivating self-awareness is vital to enhancing our financial EQ and overcoming barriers to financial growth. By identifying and addressing limiting beliefs or behaviors, we can proactively reshape our mindset and emotional relationship with money. This process involves introspection, reflection, and a willingness to challenge ingrained beliefs that no longer serve us. As we develop greater emotional intelligence concerning money, we empower ourselves to make more informed financial decisions, pursue our goals with confidence, and ultimately achieve greater financial well-being. Coupling our money EQ with greater financial literacy (money IQ) allows us to explore more opportunities for financial success.

APPLYING A GROWTH MINDSET TO FINANCIAL LITERACY

At its core, a growth mindset is not merely a belief but a guiding principle that shapes our approach to challenges and opportunities. In finance, it opens the door to possibility, illuminating a path towards financial growth and empowerment. Rather than succumbing to the notion of fixed limitations, individuals with a growth mindset understand that their financial situation is ever changing and can be influenced by their actions and choices. They embrace the idea that financial success is not solely determined by innate talent or luck but by their willingness to learn, adapt, and persevere.

In finance, a growth mindset fosters a proactive and empowered attitude towards managing money. It instills a sense of agency and responsibility, empowering individuals to take control of their financial future. Instead of resigning themselves to circumstances beyond their control, they actively seek out opportunities for growth and improvement. Whether it's learning about investing, budgeting, or entrepreneurship, they approach financial education with enthusiasm and curiosity, knowing that every lesson learned brings them closer to their financial goals.

Setbacks and challenges are inevitable on the journey to financial success, but individuals with a growth mindset embrace them as opportunities for learning and development. Rather than viewing setbacks as insurmountable obstacles or signs of personal inadequacy, they see them as valuable lessons that contribute to their growth and resilience. With each setback overcome, they emerge stronger, wiser, and more equipped to manage what lies ahead.

THE BRIDGE TO DISCOVERING YOUR FINANCIAL DREAMS

Once you recognize that what you were raised to believe about money and your ability to be successful with it greatly impacts your financial future, you can take corrective measures to release any negative beliefs that no longer serve you. This is important before you dive into setting financial goals because if you don't believe you will reach a certain salary level because your father never did or that rich people are bad because of what you have seen in the news, you are not likely to set goals that stretch you. Eliminate limiting beliefs so you can design the financial life you deserve.

Also, before setting goals, it's important to take a moment to think about what you really want to achieve. This self-reflective process lays the foundation for creating goals that are not only doable but also meaningful and satisfying. What follows are some helpful principles to help you uncover your financial dreams and pave the way for setting SMART goals (in the next chapter).

Get Clear on Your Values and Priorities—Start by pinpointing your core values and priorities in life. What matters most to you? Is it financial security, freedom, family, personal growth, or something else? Understanding your values gives you a sense of direction when setting goals that truly align with what you care about. It is also easier to say no to disruptors when you are clear on your values and priorities. Being clear becomes a decision-making tool—if it is in alignment, you can pursue it.

Define Your Long-Term Vision—Imagine your ideal financial future. What does success look like to you? Envision the lifestyle you want, whether it's owning a home, traveling the world, retiring early, or supporting your loved ones. Remember to be open to the opportunities that await you. This long-term vision acts as a guiding light for your goal-setting process.

Set Specific Objectives—Break down your long-term vision into specific, actionable objectives. What practical steps can you take to get closer to your desired financial outcomes? Whether it's paying off debt, saving for a down payment, investing for retirement, or starting a business, being clear about your objectives will help you achieve goals that are both attainable and meaningful.

Prioritize Your Goals—It's tempting to pursue multiple goals all at once, but it's important to prioritize and focus your efforts. Consider which goals are most urgent or have the biggest impact on your overall financial well-being. By prioritizing your goals, you can allocate your resources and attention more effectively.

Consider Your Resources and Limitations—Be realistic about your resources, including your income, savings, time, and skills. Take into account any constraints or challenges that might affect your ability to achieve certain goals. While it's great to aim high, setting goals that are overly ambitious or unrealistic can lead to frustration and discouragement.

Adopt a Growth Mindset—Develop a mindset of growth and resilience as you traverse your financial journey. Embrace challenges as opportunities for learning and growth, and view setbacks as temporary hurdles rather than insurmountable obstacles. By adopting a growth mindset, you empower yourself to overcome challenges and stay motivated in pursuit of your goals.

Strive for Balance—Lastly, aim for balance in your approach to goal-setting. While it's important to pursue financial goals, don't neglect other important aspects of your life, such as relationships, health, and personal fulfillment. Strive for a well-rounded approach to goal-setting that reflects your values and priorities in all areas of your life.

Discovering your financial dreams is the first step in setting SMART goals that propel you toward success and fulfillment. By clarifying your values, defining your long-term vision, setting specific objectives, prioritizing your goals, considering your resources, adopting a growth mindset, and striving for balance, you can chart a course toward a brighter financial future.

EXAMPLE IN ACTION: LIZ'S MINDSET JOURNEY

Picture Liz, a young woman whose earliest memories of money were tainted by the sound of her parents' heated arguments echoing through the house. She'd often find herself huddled in her room, trying to drown out the raised voices with her favorite toys. Those arguments left a lasting impression on Liz, imprinting in her mind the idea that money was a source of strife and tension in relationships.

As Liz grew older, this belief continued to shape her approach to money. She found herself avoiding financial success, subconsciously fearing that accumulating wealth would lead to the same discord she witnessed as a child. Whenever Liz received a raise or unexpected windfall, she couldn't shake the feeling of unease. In a bid to distance herself from the discomfort, she would impulsively spend the money on fleeting pleasures, ensuring it wouldn't linger long enough to cause trouble.

However, as Liz embarked on her journey of self-discovery, she began to realize the detrimental effects of her avoidance tactics. She understood that her fear of money was holding her back from achieving her full potential. With a newfound determination, Liz decided to challenge her old beliefs and embrace a new perspective.

A NEW MONEY MODEL

Drawing inspiration from a romantic getaway with her partner, Liz had an epiphany. She saw how money, when used wisely, could enhance experiences and bring joy into her life. Instead of associating money with conflict, Liz started to view it as a tool for adventure and connection. She envisioned a future where financial abundance would enable her to create unforgettable memories with her loved ones.

With this shift in mindset, Liz began to approach money with optimism and intention. She set goals not just for financial stability but for moments of fun and spontaneity. Whether it was planning a weekend getaway or trying out a new hobby, Liz saw every dollar as an opportunity to enrich her life and deepen her relationships.

As Liz embraced her newfound belief in the abundance of possibilities, she noticed positive changes unfolding in her life. She felt empowered to take control of her finances, knowing that her past experiences no longer defined her future. With each step forward, Liz embodied the essence of a growth mindset, embracing challenges as opportunities for growth and resilience.

In Liz's journey, money ceased to be a source of fear and became a catalyst for joy and fulfillment. She learned that by changing her beliefs, she could transform her relationship with money and unlock a world of endless possibilities. With her newfound mindset, Liz began living a life of financial empower-ment, one adventure at a time.

[2]

YOUR GUIDE TO SMART FINANCIAL GOALS

SETTING FINANCIAL GOALS is essential for anyone embarking on their financial journey. By establishing clear objectives, you give yourself direction and motivation to achieve financial success. If you don't know where you want to go or what you want to achieve, you are likely to wander through life with no particular destination and murky results.

One effective method for setting these goals is to follow the SMART criteria. SMART stands for Specific, Measurable, Achievable, Relevant, and Time-bound. Let's break down each component and see how they can be applied in a financial context.

SPECIFIC

When setting financial goals, be specific about what you want to achieve. Vague goals like "save money" or "invest in stocks" lack clarity and can make it challenging to create a plan. Instead, specify exactly what you want to accomplish. For example, rather than saying, "Save money," you could say, "Save $20,000 for a down payment on a house." Being specific helps you focus your efforts and makes it easier to track your progress.

MEASURABLE

Measurable goals are those that you can quantify. This means attaching a number or metric to your goal so you can track your progress over time. For instance, if your goal is to pay off debt, specify the exact amount you want to eliminate, such as "pay off $10,000 in credit card debt." Having a measurable goal allows you to monitor your achievements and adjust your strategies if necessary.

ACHIEVABLE

An achievable goal is one that is realistic and within reach. While it's important to aim high, setting goals that are too lofty can lead to frustration and disappointment. Consider your financial situation, resources, and abilities when setting your goals. For example, if you're just starting to invest, setting a goal to earn a 100% return on your investments in a year might not be realistic. Instead, aim for a more attainable target, such as a 7% annual return. Setting achievable goals increases your chances of success and keeps you motivated along the way.

RELEVANT

Relevant goals are those that align with your values, priorities, and long-term objectives. Before setting a financial goal, consider whether it's truly meaningful to you. Ask yourself how achieving this goal will contribute to your overall financial well-being and happiness. For instance, if your long-term goal is to retire early, investing in a high-risk, high-reward stock might not be relevant, as it could jeopardize your retirement savings. Ensure that your goals are relevant to your financial aspirations and avoid pursuing objectives that don't align with your values.

TIME-BOUND

Time-bound goals have a specific deadline or timeframe for completion. Without a deadline, it's easy to procrastinate and lose sight of your objectives. By setting a timeline, you create a sense of urgency and hold yourself accountable for taking action. For example, rather than saying, "Someday I'll start saving for retirement," set a specific deadline, such as "Start contributing to a retirement account by the end of this quarter." Having a time-bound goal helps you prioritize your financial tasks and ensures that you make steady progress toward your objectives.

There you have it; setting SMART financial goals is important in achieving financial success. By being Specific, Measurable, Achievable, Relevant, and Time-bound, you can create clear objectives that guide your actions and keep you motivated along your financial journey. Whether you're saving for a down payment on a house, paying off debt, or investing for retirement, applying the SMART criteria can help you turn your financial aspirations into reality.

EXAMPLE IN ACTION: EMILY AND JOHN

Meet Emily and John, a young couple eager to start their lives together. They shared a dream of owning a cozy home where they could start their family. But, like many of us, they felt overwhelmed by the sheer size of their goal. It felt like wishing upon a star—beautiful but distant.

Emily and John's journey started on a rainy Saturday evening. Sitting in their small apartment, they dreamed about a house with a backyard for their future kids and a kitchen big enough for Emily's baking adventures. But with their modest income and the ever-mounting living expenses, this dream seemed more like a fantasy.

THE TURNING POINT: DISCOVERING SMART GOALS

One day, John stumbled upon the concept of SMART goals during a personal finance workshop. Excited, he shared this with Emily, and they decided to try it. They wanted their goal to be **Specific**: a three-bedroom house in a nice neighborhood. They worked out they needed $40,000 for a down payment. This was their **Measurable** target.

The couple then faced the big question: Was this goal **Achievable**? They meticulously reviewed their finances, cut unnecessary expenses, and even started a side hustle. They calculated they could realistically save $1,100 each month. It wasn't easy, but it was possible.

For Emily and John, this goal was not just about a house but building a future they'd love. This made their goal incredibly **Relevant** to them. Every time they felt discouraged, they reminded each other of the cozy family dinners and the laughter-filled game nights that awaited them in their future home.

They set a **Time-Bound** target of three years, which motivated them to stay on track. They marked their progress on a big calendar in the kitchen, each month bringing them closer to their dream.

Three years later, Emily and John achieved what had once seemed impossible. They celebrated the purchase of their new home with friends and family. It was more than a house; it was evidence of their determination, a space to grow their family, and a place to make a lifetime of memories.

If Emily and John can do this, so can you. By establishing SMART goals, you can accomplish anything in a very short period of time.

[3]

BUDGETING AND
EXPENSE MANAGEMENT

CRAFTING A GOOD BUDGET is like having a map for your money. It helps you decide where your money should go so you can reach your goals. Instead of feeling stuck, you're in control. You know what you can spend and save, making it easier to achieve your financial dreams.

THE POWER OF BUDGETING

Budgeting isn't just about tracking your spending; it's about creating a plan for your money. When you budget, you're making intentional decisions about how you use your income. By understanding where your money goes, you can prioritize what's important to you and cut back on unimportant things.

Everyone benefits from budgeting, regardless of their income level. Whether you're a recent graduate starting your first job or a seasoned professional planning for retirement, a budget helps you manage your finances effectively. It provides a clear picture of your financial health and lets you make informed decisions about your spending and saving habits.

BUDGET STRUCTURES

A budget can take many forms, depending on your needs and preferences. Some people prefer a simple spreadsheet or notebook to manually track their income and expenses. Others may opt for budgeting apps or online tools that automate the process and provide real-time insights into their financial situation. Whatever method you choose, the key is finding a system that works for you that you will use regularly and stick with.

A budget typically includes categories for various expenses such as housing, transportation, groceries, entertainment, and savings. These categories help you organize your spending and identify areas to cut back if needed. Budgeting isn't about depriving yourself; it's about making conscious choices that align with your financial goals and values.

Tools like Monarch Money, YNAB (You Need a Budget), or PocketGuard can help you create and manage your budget more efficiently. As of this writing, these apps sync with your bank accounts and credit cards, categorize your transactions, and provide insights into your spending patterns. They can also send alerts when you exceed your budget limits or when it's time to pay bills or save for specific goals. There are pros and cons to each of the budgeting apps, so research them and find the best fit for you (consider sites like Forbes.com and Fortune.com for "best of" lists).

You don't have to pay for an app to build a budget. You can use a spreadsheet application that may already be on your computer and apply a template to set up a simple budget. Your bank may also have budgeting options available through their online portal or banking app.

Budgeting is a powerful financial management tool that benefits everyone. By creating a budget and using tools to track your spending, you can take control of your finances and work towards achieving your long-term goals.

CREATING A SIMPLE BUDGET

1. **Track Your Money**: Start by writing down all the money you bring in and spend, even the small stuff. This helps you understand your finances better.
2. **Sort Your Spending**: Group your spending into categories like food, fun, rent/mortgage, internet, travel, etc. This will help you see where you can spend less.
3. **Set Limits**: Decide how much you can spend in each group based on your income and

your goals. What do you want to do more of? What are you willing to spend less on to achieve your goals?

4. **Prioritize Savings and Debt Repayment:** Make saving money and paying off debt a top priority in your budget. Treat them as non-negotiable categories. This will help you build a strong financial foundation.

5. **Check and Change Regularly**: Your budget isn't set in stone; it should be a living document. Check it often and make changes as needed. Your money and goals may change, so your budget should too.

In short, mastering budgeting and managing expenses helps you take control of your finances. By making a clear plan for your money, you're on the path to reaching your financial goals, whether it's buying a home, traveling the world, or enjoying a comfortable retirement.

EXAMPLE IN ACTION: SARA'S BUDGET OVERHAUL

Sara, a graphic designer, struggled with saving money. Even when she told herself she would set aside savings at the end of the month, she often had more month than money and no savings to show for it. Talking with one of her friends over coffee one day, she lamented about her poor savings track record.

"I don't get it," Sara said. "I make good money with what I do; why can't I save any money?"

"Do you have a budget?" her friend asked.

"No."

"Then how are you going to know where your money is going? Create a simple budget so you can decide where you want your money to go."

Sara started tracking her income and expenses at her friend's suggestion, categorizing her spending, and setting limits for each category. Sara prioritized her student loan repayment and created a separate savings category for an emergency fund. By reviewing her budget monthly, she identified unnecessary expenses ("Maybe I don't need to go out for coffee every day," she reasoned) and gradually increased her savings. It felt good to see her savings grow each month. Within a year, Sara paid off a significant portion of her loan and built a sizable emergency fund.

Sara's journey shows that effective budgeting and expense management can set you up for financial stability and growth. Understanding and controlling where your money goes allows you to make informed decisions that align with your financial goals. In the next chapter, we'll address the importance of regular saving, a vital component of wealth accumulation.

[4]

MAKING REGULAR
SAVING A PRIORITY

SAVING IS OFTEN LIKENED to a foundation in the architecture of wealth creation. It's essential, yes, but it's just the beginning. Imagine it as the base of a towering skyscraper. It provides stability and security, a starting point. But on its own, more is needed to reach the lofty heights of substantial wealth. Savings act as a buffer, a financial safety net that cushions you against life's unexpected tumbles. Yet, this safety net is just one layer of a multi-tiered approach to wealth building.

The real journey to wealth extends beyond the comfort of accumulating savings. Consider it the first step on a ladder. It would be best to have more than this to climb to the top—like strategic investing, smart budgeting, and effective debt management. For example, when building a house, after laying the foundation, you need to erect walls, install a roof, and set up essential systems like plumbing, electrical, and heating. In financial terms, these are your investments, retirement plans, and diversified income streams. They're what turn a solid base into a thriving, prosperous structure.

HOW MUCH TO SAVE: FINDING YOUR FINANCIAL EQUILIBRIUM

Determining the right amount to save is akin to calibrating a delicate machine. The consensus among many financial experts is to aim for an emergency fund covering around six months of living expenses. This fund acts like a buffer, a financial cushion that absorbs the shocks of life's unpredictable twists—sudden job loss, an unexpected medical emergency, or other unforeseen expenses.

This emergency fund is like having a well-stocked pantry in times of need—it provides peace of mind and a sense of security. But it's also important not to overfill your pantry at the expense of other opportunities. Once you've established this security baseline, it's time to look beyond. It's about finding that sweet spot where your savings are sufficient to cover emergencies but not so excessive that they hinder your ability to grow wealth.

Investment is the next stage of this financial journey. Unlike a savings account, investments can flourish and multiply, offering opportunities for significant wealth accumulation. This phase, which we'll cover later in the book, explores various avenues, such as stocks, bonds, real estate, mutual funds, and retirement accounts. Each of these avenues presents its risks and rewards, and the key lies in finding the right mix that aligns with your financial goals and risk tolerance.

THE ART OF CREATING THE HABIT: EMBEDDING FINANCIAL DISCIPLINE

Forming a savings habit requires embedding a new, positive routine into your life. Research indicates a new habit takes twenty-one to forty-five days to take root. This period is critical; it's where the seeds of your future financial stability are sown. The focus should be on small, manageable actions in the early days. It might mean setting aside a fixed percentage of each paycheck into a savings account or cutting back on certain luxuries. The goal during this initial period is not to amass a large savings balance overnight but to cultivate a regular, disciplined practice of saving.

The emphasis in these first few weeks should be on the regularity of your saving actions. Think of it as training for a marathon. You start with short runs, gradually building up stamina and distance. Similarly, saving is about building financial stamina—the ability to consistently set aside money, no matter how small the amount. Over time, these regular deposits, much like the consistent training runs, build up to something substantial. (And it is fun to watch it grow.)

During this initial period, a psychological transformation also occurs. It's about shifting your mindset to view saving not as a burdensome task but as an empowering and positive financial habit. Celebrating small victories is vital—each time you see your savings grow, even by a small amount, it reinforces your commitment to this new habit.

As this saving habit solidifies, it influences other areas of your financial life. You become more mindful of your spending, more strategic in your budgeting, and more thoughtful in your financial decision-making. Over time, this disciplined approach to saving can build a significant financial reserve, providing both security and a sense of accomplishment.

SETTING CLEAR SAVINGS GOALS: CHARTING YOUR FINANCIAL JOURNEY

Setting clear savings goals is much like plotting a course on a map. Without a clear destination, you might wander. Specific goals transform the nebulous idea of saving money into a concrete, achievable target. Whether saving for a near-term desire like a new gadget or a long-term aspiration like a home down payment, having a defined objective gives purpose and direction to your savings efforts.

Think of each dollar saved as a step toward your goal. This approach makes the act of saving more intentional and rewarding. Instead of aimlessly accumulating money, you're working towards something tangible—a vacation, a new car, an investment account, or a college fund for your kids. Tie this to the goals you created earlier in this book. This approach turns the sometimes monotonous process of saving into an exciting and meaningful endeavor.

Some experts suggest having multiple savings accounts to use for specific purposes like education/personal development, investments, contributions, and long-term savings for major expenditures. Author T. Harv Eker even suggests having a "play" account that holds a small percentage of money that you will spend each month or quarter just for fun. Remember, the goal is not to hoard your money and take the fun out of life but to give you control of your money so you can live life to the fullest.

ADAPTING YOUR SAVING HABITS: CULTIVATING FINANCIAL AGILITY

Like learning a new skill or hobby, adapting your saving habits might feel unfamiliar and challenging at first, but with practice, it becomes a natural part of your routine. Regular saving is a foundational element of effective money management. It supports other aspects of your financial health, acting as a stepping stone to more complex and rewarding financial strategies.

As you continue to save, you learn to adjust and adapt your habits to match your evolving financial situation and goals. You could start by saving a small percentage of your income, then gradually increase it as you become more comfortable and financially stable. Or you could find creative ways to cut expenses, boosting your ability to save without significantly impacting your lifestyle. (Each time you decide not to go out for that smoothie, you can put what you would have spent in your savings account.) Over time, these adapted saving habits form the cornerstone of your broader financial strategy, supporting your journey toward wealth creation and financial independence.

Example in Action: Mia's Savings Transformation and Journey of Financial Growth

Mia went from being an occasional saver to a disciplined financial planner. Initially, the concept of saving regularly seemed daunting. She didn't learn about saving as a child; she always spent the money she received in birthday cards, and her parents didn't tell her to do any different. She didn't even have a savings account in her formative years.

Now, after being on her own for years and having friends with a positive money mindset, Mia made the decision to create a savings account and set a concrete goal—a professional writing course that would advance her career. This goal gave her savings efforts a clear direction. She began by making small, manageable changes, such as not buying every new gadget as soon as it came out, automating her savings by having five percent of her income automatically transferred from her checking account every two weeks, and carefully tracking her expenses.

Over six months, these small steps culminated in a substantial achievement. Not only had Mia saved enough for the course, but she had also ingrained a strong saving habit. This new discipline extended into other aspects of her financial life, leading to more thoughtful spending and a greater sense of control over her finances. She decided to make her money a source of expansion and joy. That's the transformative power of regular saving. It's a journey that starts with a single step and, over time, leads to a path of financial stability and empowerment.

[5]

DISTINCT APPROACHES TO WEALTH

FINDING INSPIRATION FROM effective financial strategies can help you achieve financial independence and build wealth. It's not just about making random investments; it's about adopting a comprehensive understanding and mimicking the habits and strategies employed by those who have successfully grown their wealth. In this chapter, we'll examine how different groups, such as business professionals, millionaires, and the elite, approach wealth creation, each with their unique methods and areas of focus. Discover what sets these successful individuals apart and how to apply their insights to our financial goals.

BUSINESS PROFESSIONALS AND EXECUTIVES: THE EARNING FOCUS

Business professionals and executives earn significantly more than average, especially those at the top of corporate hierarchies or in pivotal roles. A key aspect of their financial success lies in their focus on generating personal income through relentless hard work and innovative thinking. Their strategic approach to wealth involves dedicating approximately 70% of their focus to personal income generation. This doesn't just mean working harder; it's about working smarter, identifying and leveraging opportunities for growth within their professional sphere.

Beyond their own efforts, these professionals allocate about 25% of their time to strategies enabling others to generate income for them. This could include wise investment decisions, where money is placed into ventures or stocks with the potential for high returns, or hiring skilled individuals who can contribute to their financial goals. They understand that personal effort, while paramount, can be significantly amplified through smart delegation and investment.

The remaining 5% of their focus is particularly interesting. It is devoted to understanding and optimizing their *rate of return*. This means they are not just passively investing in stocks or real estate; they are actively involved in ensuring each investment is as fruitful as possible. This could involve meticulous market research, consulting with financial experts, or diversifying their investment portfolios to mitigate risks and maximize returns.

MILLIONAIRES: BALANCING EARNING AND INVESTING

Millionaires' approaches often differ slightly. While they still value direct income generation, they spend only 20% of their time on it. A substantial 60% of their focus is on leveraging how others can contribute to their wealth. This could mean investing in other people's businesses, funding startups with the potential for high returns, or employing financial experts to identify lucrative investment opportunities that might be overlooked.

The remaining 20% of their time is dedicated to seeking powerful growth avenues. This includes investments like property acquisitions, which can provide rental income and long-term capital gains, or business development, where they might expand their businesses or start new ventures. This strategy shows a balanced approach between earning, leveraging others' efforts, and investing in growth opportunities.

THE ELITE CLASS: MAXIMIZING INVESTMENT RETURNS

The elite class, comprising the super-rich, exhibits a distinct approach. They spend only about 5% of their time on direct earning activities. For them, the primary focus is not on generating income through traditional means but on wealth multiplication. They allocate 35% to understanding and strategizing how others can contribute to their wealth. This could involve complex investment strategies, funding large-scale projects, or engaging in high-level networking to find unique investment opportunities.

A significant 60% of their focus is on investment strategies to multiply their wealth. This involves high-stakes investments in substantial projects, exploring international markets, or finding innovative and efficient ways to make their money work harder for them. Their approach is less about active income generation and more about strategic, often passive, wealth multiplication.

EXAMPLE IN ACTION: CHARTING YOUR WEALTH PATH

Let's consider a practical example to illustrate how these principles can be applied in everyday life. Maria, a mid-level manager, finds inspiration in these wealth-creation strategies. Realizing the importance of earning and growing wealth, she decides to dedicate more time to understanding investments and exploring opportunities beyond her conventional job.

Starting small, Maria invests in a mix of stocks and mutual funds. As her confidence and knowledge grow, she gradually increases the diversity of her investment portfolio, venturing into more complex and potentially more rewarding investments. Recognizing the value of experiential learning, Maria joins a real estate investment group. Here, she gains firsthand investment experience and learns from seasoned investors, aligning her approach closer to that of the millionaire mindset.

Maria's journey underscores a critical lesson: adopting a mindset focused on earning and smartly growing your wealth is essential for financial success. Notably, one doesn't need to start with substantial wealth to think and act like these successful individuals. The focus should be a balanced mix of earning, saving, and especially investing wisely. It's not just about making money; it's about making your money make more money. It's about planting the seeds for your financial growth and nurturing them consistently through strategic planning, continuous learning, and adapting to the ever-changing financial environment.

Drawing inspiration from successful financial strategies involves understanding and applying the differentiated approaches of various wealth-creating groups. From the earning-focused strategies of business professionals and executives to the balanced approach of millionaires and the investment-centric focus of the elite class, each group offers valuable insights into wealth creation. By adopting these strategies, individuals can embark on a path of financial growth, learning from the successes of those who have mastered the art of wealth accumulation.

[6]

Understanding
Credit: Like It or Not

CREDIT IS A CORNERSTONE of modern finance, essential for both personal and business success. Individuals and entrepreneurs can make savvy financial decisions by understanding the various types of credit—such as personal credit cards, business lines of credit, and more—along with their unique benefits and potential pitfalls. This chapter touches on the intricacies of credit, empowering you to manage your financial journey with confidence and clarity.

What is Credit?

At its core, credit is an agreement between a borrower and a lender that allows the borrower to obtain goods, services, or money now, based on the promise to repay the lender at a later date. This arrangement is built on trust, where the lender trusts the borrower to fulfill their repayment obligation.

When a lender extends credit to a borrower, they assess the borrower's ability to repay. This assessment evaluates various factors, such as the borrower's credit history, income, and overall financial health. Credit terms include the amount borrowed, the interest rate, the repayment schedule, and any associated fees.

Interest is a key component of credit. It is the cost of borrowing money and is usually expressed as an annual percentage rate (APR). The borrower must repay the principal amount (the original amount borrowed) along with interest, which compensates the lender for the risk and opportunity cost of lending money.

You should also note that other companies you do business with may rely on your strong credit history to provide services to you, even though you are not borrowing money from them. For example, when you apply for an apartment or house to rent or establish utilities for your new home, a strong credit history provides greater confidence that you will honor your financial obligations (i.e., pay the rent). When you travel, renting a car and securing a hotel room may also require credit. Thus, building and maintaining a good credit history is important to function in our current economy.

CREDITWORTHINESS

Creditworthiness measures your ability to repay debt and is assessed by lenders using credit scores and credit reports. Consistently paying bills on time is one of the most critical factors in boosting your creditworthiness. Late payments can significantly harm your credit score.

Credit utilization, which is the ratio of your current credit balances to your credit limits (or what you owe versus what is available to you), should be kept low—preferably below 30%. A longer credit history generally improves your credit score, as it provides more information about your financial behavior. Having a mix of different types of credit, like credit cards, installment loans, and mortgages, can also positively impact your credit score.

Finally, frequently opening new credit accounts can be seen as risky behavior and can lower your credit score. Understanding and managing these factors allows you to build and maintain a strong credit profile, opening up opportunities for better loan terms, lower interest rates, and greater financial flexibility.

TYPES OF CREDIT

PERSONAL CREDIT

Personal credit refers to the ability of an individual to borrow money or access goods and services with the understanding that payment will be made in the future. Personal credit comes in various forms, including:

1. Credit Cards: A common form of revolving credit where users can borrow up to a certain limit and repay over time, usually with interest.

2. Installment Loans: Loans such as auto loans or personal loans in which the borrower repays the loan in fixed monthly payments over a specified period.

3. Mortgages: Long-term loans used to purchase real estate, typically repaid over 15 to 30 years with interest.

BUSINESS CREDIT

Business credit is a business's ability to obtain financing. It is separate from personal credit and based on the business's financial health.

1. Business Credit Cards: Similar to personal credit cards but issued to businesses. They often come with business-specific perks, such as higher credit limits and rewards for business expenditures.

2. Lines of Credit: Provide businesses with flexible access to funds up to a certain limit, which they can draw from as needed, repay, and borrow again.

3. Term Loans: Fixed amount of capital lenders provide that businesses repay with interest over a set period.
4. Trade Credit: An agreement where a business can purchase goods and pay the supplier at a later date.

SEPARATING PERSONAL AND BUSINESS FINANCES AND CREDIT

One of the foundational principles for managing business finances effectively is separating personal and business finances and credit. This distinction is important for several reasons, including risk mitigation, estate planning, and a business's overall financial health.

RISK MITIGATION

When personal and business finances are intertwined, it becomes challenging to assess the financial health of either accurately. By keeping them separate, you can better track business expenses and revenues to create reliable financial statements. This separation also protects personal assets from business liabilities. If the business incurs debt or faces legal action, personal assets such as your home or savings are shielded from claims by creditors.

Additionally, separate finances simplify tax preparation. Businesses have different tax obligations compared to individuals. Keeping finances separate ensures that business deductions are not missed and personal expenses are not mistakenly deducted, which could lead to penalties or audits.

ESTATE PLANNING

From an estate planning perspective, maintaining separate finances can make the process of transferring business ownership smoother. If personal and business assets are entangled, it complicates the division of assets among heirs or beneficiaries. A clearly defined separation ensures the business can be valued and transferred independently of personal assets, facilitating a smoother ownership transition.

In the event of an unexpected death, clear separation aids in the efficient settlement of the estate. It ensures the business can continue operating without financial confusion, providing stability for employees and other stakeholders.

ESTABLISHING, EVALUATING, AND SELLING A BUSINESS

Having a separate business credit profile is important when establishing a business. It allows the business to build its own credit history independent of the owner's personal credit. Lenders will evaluate the business's creditworthiness rather than the owner's credit score when seeking financing.

Clear financial separation provides an accurate picture of the business's financial health for valuation purposes. Investors and potential buyers require transparent financial statements to assess the business's value and performance. Accurate and separate records increase the credibility of financial reports, making the business more attractive to investors.

Having distinct personal and business finances simplifies the due diligence process when selling a business. Potential buyers can easily review the business's financial records without sifting through personal transactions. This transparency can expedite the sale process and potentially increase the business's valuation.

GOING PUBLIC

If a business plans to go public (sell shares of ownership to the public in exchange for cash), maintaining separate finances is indispensable. Public companies are subject to rigorous financial scrutiny and regulatory requirements. Clear separation ensures compliance with financial reporting standards and builds investor confidence. It also simplifies the auditing process, as auditors can verify the business's financial records without personal financial data complicating the review.

Maintaining distinct personal and business finances is not just about organization; it's about protecting your personal assets, ensuring smooth business operations, and laying the groundwork for future financial opportunities. Understanding and implementing this separation is a fundamental step in effectively managing both personal and business financial health.

HOW TO ESTABLISH CREDIT

Effective debt management for wealth accumulation involves a two-pronged approach: focusing on income-producing debt and emphasizing asset accumulation. These principles form the cornerstone of effective debt management for wealth accumulation.

PERSONAL CREDIT

Establishing personal credit helps you build a solid financial foundation. Start by opening a checking or savings account. This demonstrates financial responsibility and can serve as your gateway to other financial products.

Next, consider applying for a secured credit card, especially if you're new to credit. With a secured card, you deposit money as collateral, which typically serves as your credit limit. Use this card for small purchases and make sure to pay off the balance each month. This will help you build a positive credit history and show creditworthiness.

Another option is to become an authorized user on a family member or friend's credit card. This means you get a card in your name, but the primary account holder is responsible for the payments. If the primary cardholder uses the card responsibly, it can positively impact your credit score.

Paying your bills on time is also important. Late payments can severely damage your credit score. Set up automatic payments or reminders to avoid missing due dates. Lastly, regularly check your credit report from the three major credit bureaus: Equifax, Experian, and TransUnion. This helps ensure all information is accurate and allows you to address discrepancies promptly. In the US, you can access your credit report for free every twelve months (see the Consumer Financial Protection Bureau website for details).

BUSINESS CREDIT

Building business credit is essential for keeping your personal and business finances separate and for accessing funding opportunities. Start by formally registering your business as a limited liability company (LLC), corporation, or partnership, and obtain an Employer Identification Number (EIN) from the IRS. This establishes your business as a separate legal entity.

Open a business checking account to handle all business transactions. This helps maintain a clear distinction between personal and business finances. Next, apply for a business credit card. Use this card responsibly and pay off the balance each month to build a positive credit history for your business.

Establishing trade lines with vendors who report to business credit bureaus is another important step. Ensure you pay your invoices on time to build a strong credit profile. Regularly check your business credit report from agencies like Dun & Bradstreet, Experian Business, and Equifax Business. This will help you keep track of your business's credit status and correct any inaccuracies.

CREDIT BUREAUS AND THE ROLE OF DUN & BRADSTREET

Credit bureaus play a primary role in collecting and maintaining credit information. The three major credit bureaus for personal credit are Equifax, Experian, and TransUnion. These agencies compile credit reports based on your financial behavior, including payment history, credit utilization, and the length of your credit history.

In the business world, major credit reporting agencies include Dun & Bradstreet (D&B), Experian Business, and Equifax Business. Dun & Bradstreet is particularly important. They assign each business a unique nine-digit identifier, known as the D-U-N-S Number. This number is widely used to identify and track a company's credit history.

D&B collects and analyzes business information to produce credit scores and ratings, such as the PAYDEX score, which reflects a business's payment performance. These ratings help lenders, suppliers, and partners assess the risk of doing business with a company. D&B's comprehensive business credit reports include financial statements, payment history, and public records, which lenders use to make informed credit decisions.

You can access financing and build strong business relationships by monitoring and maintaining good credit with these bureaus.

WHY CREDIT IS SO IMPORTANT TODAY

In today's financial world, credit is more important than ever. It's the lifeline that enables significant investments, like buying a home, starting a business, or funding education. Without credit, making large purchases and spreading out payments over time would be much harder, and managing cash flow would be a real challenge.

Credit also drives economic growth. When consumers use credit to buy goods and services, it boosts production and stimulates economic activity. For businesses, credit is the fuel that powers expansion, job creation, and innovation. It's a critical tool for investing in new opportunities and staying competitive.

Building a good credit history is another vital aspect. A solid credit record opens doors to more services like home and car rentals, better loan terms, lower interest rates, and higher credit limits. This can lead to significant savings and more financial flexibility over time. A good credit score can greatly affect your financial health and activity.

Credit isn't just for planned expenses; it's a safety net during emergencies. Unexpected costs like medical bills or urgent repairs can be managed without disrupting your financial stability. Having access to credit provides peace of mind, knowing you can handle unforeseen expenses.

Credit is indispensable for smooth operations for businesses. It helps manage cash flow, invest in inventory, and cover operating expenses during slower periods. Moreover, business credit can be the key to seizing growth opportunities, whether expanding to new markets or developing new products.

Credit also allows individuals and businesses to act on opportunities that require immediate funding. Whether it's jumping on a limited-time offer, investing in the stock market, or pursuing business expansion, credit provides the necessary capital to act quickly and strategically.

Credit is essential for international trade and commerce in our interconnected global economy. It helps businesses bridge the gap between paying suppliers and receiving customer payments, which is necessary for maintaining liquidity and stability.

Understanding the critical role of credit helps individuals and businesses use it wisely.

EXAMPLE IN ACTION: ALEX'S JOURNEY TO BUILDING CREDIT

Alex, a recent college graduate, was eager to start his professional life on the right foot. He knew that understanding credit was crucial, but like many, he was initially clueless about where to begin. With a diploma in hand and a new job in a bustling city, Alex decided it was time to dive into the world of credit.

His first step was opening a checking and savings account at a local bank. This seemed simple enough but was a foundational move demonstrating his financial responsibility. Encouraged by this small success, Alex then applied for a secured credit card. He deposited $500 as collateral, which became his credit limit. With this card, Alex began making small purchases for essentials like groceries and gas, ensuring he paid off the balance in full every month. This responsible behavior was his first foray into building a positive credit history.

Wanting to boost his credit profile further, Alex spoke to his parents about becoming an authorized user on their credit card. They agreed, adding another layer of positive credit activity to his growing credit history. His parents' excellent credit habits reflected positively on him, giving his credit score a healthy boost. This helped him secure a lease on a great new apartment near his place of work.

Alex was diligent about monitoring his credit reports. He took advantage of the free annual reports from Equifax, Experian, and TransUnion to ensure accurate information. He staggered the free reports from each bureau every four months to monitor his credit all year (avoiding the cost of a credit monitoring service). This regular check-up helped him quickly catch and resolve any discrepancies, keeping his credit profile clean and accurate.

After a few years of diligently managing his personal credit, Alex felt confident enough to start his own digital marketing agency. He formally registered his business as an LLC and obtained an Employer Identification Number (EIN) from the IRS. His next step was opening a business checking account, which he used for all business-related transactions, separating his personal and business finances.

Applying for a business credit card was the next logical move. Alex used it responsibly, just as he had with his personal credit card, and paid off the balance each month. He also established trade lines with a few key vendors who reported to business credit bureaus, further building his business's credit profile.

One evening, while researching ways to strengthen his business credit, Alex learned about Dun & Bradstreet (D&B). He ensured his business obtained a D-U-N-S Number. Paying close attention to his PAYDEX score became part of his routine. Maintaining a good score meant better financing options and stronger relationships with suppliers and partners.

With a solid foundation in both personal and business credit, Alex was now ready to leverage credit to seize new opportunities. He secured a business loan with favorable terms, which allowed him to expand his agency, hire more staff, and invest in new technology. This strategic use of credit helped Alex's business grow and thrive in a competitive market.

Throughout his journey, Alex understood the importance of creditworthiness. He consistently paid bills on time, kept his credit utilization low, and maintained a mix of credit types. By doing so, Alex enhanced his credit scores and secured his financial future.

Alex's journey highlights how a clear understanding of credit and responsible financial behavior can pave the way for personal and business success. Establishing and maintaining good credit opens doors to opportunities and provides the financial flexibility needed to achieve long-term goals.

[7]

THE STRATEGIC EDGE: DEBT IN WEALTH BUILDING

WHEN WE HEAR the word debt, it usually brings up negative thoughts and makes us think of financial burdens. But in savvy wealth-building, debt takes on a different role. It becomes a powerful ally in accumulating wealth when used wisely. It's all about understanding the concept of *Other People's Money* (OPM) and leveraging it to your advantage. This strategy acknowledges that when used intelligently, strategic debt can help offset income gaps and minimize the impact of bad debts. We will dig deeper into this idea and explore the importance of distinguishing between good and bad debt. We'll also see how leveraging debt can prioritize the growth of your assets and cash flow.

Redefining Good Debt vs. Bad Debt: A Nuanced Perspective

The traditional black-and-white categorization of debt into good and bad requires a more nuanced understanding, which has strategic implications that can transform one's approach to borrowing. To aid in understanding this discussion, in simple terms, assets are things you own (that usually have some future financial benefit), and liabilities (debt) are what you owe to others, usually in the form of money.

Bad Debt—The Financial Drainer

Think of bad debts as those pesky leaks in your financial boat. These liabilities sap your financial resources without giving anything back in return. High-interest credit card debts and personal loans for consumption purposes fall into this category. They act as insidious drains on your finances, impeding your progress and limiting your growth potential.

For example, imagine a recent graduate, Emma, enticed by the allure of instant gratification. She succumbs to the temptation of credit cards, accumulating debt with each impulsive purchase: a pair of shoes, a new sofa, and a short weekend getaway. As the interest mounts and minimum payments loom, Emma finds herself trapped in a cycle of financial struggle, her aspirations overshadowed by the burden of debt.

GOOD DEBT—THE WEALTH BUILDER

In contrast, good debt serves as a strategic tool for wealth accumulation. It's an investment in your financial future. It transcends mere borrowing, evolving into investments that propel your financial future. Think of loans for income-generating properties, business expansion, or assets poised for appreciation. Good debt is a strategic tool, not just for growth but for creating new avenues for increased cash flow and asset accumulation. It's borrowing with a purpose, with an eye on the future returns it can bring.

Let's shift our focus to James, a driven entrepreneur. Recognizing the potential in real estate, he strategically leverages a mortgage to acquire a rental property. With each rental payment, James not only services his debt but also cultivates a steady stream of passive income. Over time, as property values appreciate and rental demand surges, James' investment becomes a cornerstone of his financial portfolio, offering both stability and growth.

Understanding and using debt can feel daunting, especially for novice investors. However, armed with knowledge and a strategic mindset, you can distinguish between good and bad debt, steer clear of financial pitfalls, and embrace opportunities for growth.

STRATEGIC USE OF OPM IN WEALTH CREATION

Leverage for Asset Accumulation: Imagine OPM as a key that unlocks doors to larger assets, enhancing your investment portfolio. For instance, a mortgage for a rental property is not just a loan; it's a ticket to owning a significant asset. As we saw with James above, the income from this property can cover the debt and even contribute to your wealth-building journey.

Offsetting Income Deficiencies: Strategic debt can act as a bridge over troubled financial waters. You can counterbalance income gaps by accumulating good debts that yield positive returns. The cash flow generated from these investments can pay off the debt and even spill over to cover other expenses.

Accelerating Wealth Building: Well-managed debt can fast-track your journey to wealth accumulation. It opens doors to investment opportunities that might be out of reach with just direct income, thus multiplying your financial resources at a pace that would be impossible otherwise.

Eliminating Bad Debts: Interestingly, strategic good debt can also help mitigate the impact of bad debts. Channeling cash flow from good debts to clear liabilities can significantly improve your overall financial health.

The Art of Managing Debt for Asset Growth

Effective debt management for wealth accumulation involves a two-pronged approach: focusing on income-producing debt and emphasizing asset accumulation. These principles form the cornerstone of effective debt management for wealth accumulation.

Income-Producing Debt as the Cornerstone

The essence of using debt wisely lies in focusing on debts that fuel income generation. This means prioritizing loans invested in ventures or assets with returns that surpass the debt's cost. It's about creating a situation where the income from these investments covers the debt and adds to your financial well-being. This creates a self-sustaining cycle.

Asset Accumulation as the Ultimate Goal

Asset accumulation is the endgame of strategic debt management. This approach zeros in on building a portfolio of appreciating, income-generating assets that provide long-term stability and growth. The objective is to identify and invest in assets offering value appreciation and regular income, such as real estate, stocks, or business ventures.

Understanding and utilizing strategic debt can dramatically alter your financial portfolio. By accumulating good debts that augment cash flow and asset growth, you can transform debt from a financial burden into a potent tool in wealth accumulation. Continuously evaluating and adapting your debt strategy are essential for staying on course toward your financial goals. This may require a shift from viewing debt as a financial boogeyman to embracing it as a strategic component of your financial strategy.

EXAMPLE IN ACTION: JESSICA'S STRATEGIC DEBT APPROACH

Jessica is an entrepreneur who masterfully uses debt to grow wealth. Her journey begins with the launch of her boutique, where she gets a loan to kickstart her business. Recognizing the potential for high returns and continuous income, Jessica strategically invests in her venture, ensuring that the debt incurred is a catalyst for wealth growth rather than a burden. For instance, she secures a $50,000 loan with an 8% interest rate to finance her boutique's initial inventory and operational expenses.

However, Jessica doesn't stop there. Understanding the power of OPM, she sets her sights on real estate investment as another avenue for wealth accumulation. Leveraging a mortgage, Jessica purchases a duplex in a thriving neighborhood with the intention of converting it into a rental property. She secures a $200,000 mortgage with a 7% interest rate, with the rental income projected to cover the monthly mortgage payments and generate additional cash flow. By strategically using OPM in this manner, Jessica diversifies her investment portfolio and establishes a reliable source of passive income.

As Jessica's rental property generates steady cash flow, she reinvests the surplus funds into further expanding her business and acquiring additional income-producing assets. For example, she allocates a portion of her rental income towards renovating her boutique, attracting more customers and driving up sales. Additionally, Jessica explores other investment opportunities, such as purchasing dividend-paying stocks or investing in a small business venture, all financed through her capital and strategically acquired debt. Through her strategic approach to debt management, Jessica demonstrates how judiciously leveraging OPM can fuel wealth creation, asset accumulation, and income generation, ultimately positioning her for long-term financial success and security.

[8]

Embracing Lifelong Financial Learning

THE ARENA OF FINANCE is inherently fluid and constantly evolving. Staying informed about new developments, products, and market shifts is imperative for anyone intent on effectively creating and managing wealth. This commitment to ongoing financial education is essential for staying competitive and successful.

Grasping the Fundamentals

Building a strong financial foundation begins with understanding basic concepts. These include the different types of investments, the role of inflation, and the fundamental principles of risk and return.

Interest Rates: These represent the cost of borrowing money or the potential earnings from saving it. Understanding interest rates helps you make informed decisions about loans, mortgages, and savings.

Dividends: These are payments made to shareholders by companies from profits. They represent a return on investment and are a vital income component for many investors.

Equity: This refers to an ownership interest in an asset, like stocks in a company. It is also the difference between an asset you own and its liability. Understanding equity in stock market investments and assessing company valuations is essential.

Cash Flow: This is the net amount of cash and cash equivalents being transferred into and out of businesses or personal finances. Maintaining financial health and making strategic investments requires effective cash flow management.

DIVERSE KNOWLEDGE SOURCES AND APPLICATIONS

Diversification in learning is as important as in investing. Expand your knowledge through various channels like books, podcasts, seminars, online videos, and various financial news sources. In the Suggested Readings section of this book, we have provided a small collection of book titles for you. Continuous learning ensures a comprehensive understanding of financial principles and strategies, safeguarding against one-dimensional viewpoints.

Theoretical knowledge gains real value when applied practically. Use your growing financial understanding to refine your budgeting, adjust your investment strategies, or reassess your long-term financial goals. This practical application is key to transforming theoretical knowledge into effective financial management.

The financial world is in constant flux, shaped by global events, economic cycles, and technological innovations. Stay adaptable and responsive to these changes. It involves regularly reassessing and adjusting your financial strategies to align with the current economic climate and future projections.

THE ROLE OF FINANCIAL GOALS

Your financial goals are the compass that guides your educational pursuits. Whether you're focused on retirement planning, saving for college, or building a robust investment portfolio, tailor your learning to support and advance these objectives. Aligning your educational efforts with your financial goals ensures a focused and relevant learning experience.

Embed financial education into your routine. Dedicate regular time each week to expand your financial knowledge. This ongoing commitment is vital. In wealth management, knowledge is not just power—it's a tool for growth, stability, and success. But it has to be applied to make an impact.

EXAMPLE IN ACTION: ELLA'S EDUCATIONAL JOURNEY

Ella, a young professional, recognized the value of financial literacy early in her career. She started with the basics and progressively dug into more complex topics like investment strategies and tax planning. Her dedication to continual learning bolstered her confidence in financial management and equipped her to make informed, strategic investment choices that resonated with her long-term objectives.

But Ella also realized many in her community didn't understand financial concepts to bolster their economic conditions. So, Ella created YouTube videos to share what she was learning. Those videos went viral, and now Ella shares her financial education with others on various podcasts.

Ella's journey is a testament to the pivotal role of ongoing financial education in effective wealth management. By staying informed and consistently expanding your knowledge, you can make more astute financial decisions, adapt to market changes, and maintain a competitive edge in the rapidly changing world of finance. Sharing what you learn with others helps to solidify your learning and encourages you to stay on top. This proactive approach to financial literacy empowers you to manage your financial life, making informed decisions that align with current realities and future aspirations.

[9]

Retirement Planning Simplified

WHEN CONTEMPLATING RETIREMENT, it's common to focus primarily on saving. However, while saving is a valuable practice, it shouldn't be the sole strategy for retirement planning. Let's explore a few potential approaches to retirement planning intelligently and effectively.

Imagine retirement planning as constructing a fortress to safeguard your future financial well-being. Traditional saving is like stacking bricks, one by one, meticulously building a solid foundation. It's reliable and steady but may take time to see substantial growth. Now, let's introduce the concept of creating passive income streams—it's akin to installing a network of hidden springs that continually feed into your fortress, bolstering its strength and resilience. These springs represent investments in businesses, real estate, stocks, bonds, retirement funds, and more, carefully chosen to yield returns without requiring your direct, active involvement. While saving diligently lays the groundwork, integrating passive income sources turbocharges the growth of your retirement accounts, accelerating your journey toward financial security and independence. Just as a fortress fortified with hidden springs is better equipped to withstand the test of time, a retirement plan bolstered by passive income streams offers greater resilience and longevity in the face of life's uncertainties.

Passive Income Models

How do you establish such passive income? It involves setting up efficient systems, collaborating with the right people, and having clear agreements in your business operations. Think of it as creating an autonomous machine that operates smoothly, ensuring a steady income flow even when you're not directly involved. Examples include affiliate marketing, investing in others' businesses, and strategic alliances.

When others have established business systems that align with or complement your business or industry, creating a referral or affiliate relationship with them can be a lucrative way to generate passive income. In today's digital world, sharing another company's digital products is easy to do using lead generators, funnels, and email autoresponders. Many companies who appreciate having affiliate marketers share their products or services have the marketing materials you need to make it easy. All you have to do is plug and play.

Retirement planning isn't just about generating income. It's equally about engaging in activities you love. It doesn't feel burdensome when you're passionate about what you do. In this way, you don't "retire" from something you love; instead, you find a harmonious balance where work becomes a choice driven by desire, not necessity. For example, some keynote speakers love entertaining large crowds and traveling worldwide. They can't imagine doing anything else. Many such speakers plan to be on stage until the end because, to them, it is not work; it is sharing their passion with their audiences.

RETIREMENT ACCOUNTS: BUILDING BLOCKS FOR FINANCIAL SECURITY

Though they are less fun than traveling the world speaking on stages, retirement accounts like 401(k) plans and Roth IRAs are potent tools in retirement planning that you can tap into while employed. These tools offer distinct advantages and strategies to help individuals secure their financial futures efficiently. Once they are set up, they are relatively passive.

401(k) Plans are employer-sponsored retirement accounts that allow employees to contribute a portion of their pre-tax income, often with the added benefit of employer-matching contributions (if you are a W2 wage earner). One of the key advantages of a 401(k) plan is the tax-deferred growth it offers. Contributions are made with pre-tax dollars, meaning they reduce your taxable income in the year they're made, and the earnings in the account grow tax-deferred until withdrawal during retirement. This tax deferral can significantly accelerate the growth of your retirement savings over time.

Additionally, many employers offer matching contributions, effectively providing free money that boosts your retirement savings further. Developing an efficient system for retirement planning with a 401(k) involves maximizing contributions to take full advantage of employer matches, carefully selecting investment options tailored to your risk tolerance and retirement timeline, and periodically reassessing and adjusting your contributions and investment allocations as your financial situation evolves.

The Roth IRA is another retirement planning vehicle. Unlike 401(k) plans, Roth IRAs are individual retirement accounts funded with after-tax dollars. While contributions to a Roth IRA are not tax-deductible (talk to your tax professional for guidance), the real magic happens with withdrawals during retirement.

Qualified distributions from Roth IRAs, including contributions and earnings, are tax-free, providing tax diversification in retirement. This means you can withdraw money from your Roth IRA without worrying about paying taxes, which can be particularly advantageous if you anticipate being in a higher tax bracket during retirement or want to minimize your tax liability in retirement. Efficient retirement planning with a Roth IRA involves contributing consistently over time to maximize the tax-free growth potential, strategically converting traditional IRA or 401(k) assets to Roth IRA assets when it makes sense from a tax perspective, and carefully managing withdrawals during retirement to minimize taxes and maximize retirement income.

By leveraging the unique benefits of 401(k) plans and Roth IRAs, individuals can develop efficient retirement planning systems that optimize tax advantages, maximize investment growth, and ultimately build a solid foundation for a secure and comfortable retirement. Not everyone will have these retirement funds set up, and not all employers will contribute to them, but you should be aware that it is an option for you.

BUILDING YOUR RETIREMENT SYSTEM

So, how should you start? Begin by defining clear financial goals for your retirement. Ask yourself what you envision for retirement and how much money you'll need to achieve this lifestyle. Will you need a clothing budget for speaking attire and a travel budget to support your engagements? Do you plan to buy an RV and travel the country? Will you summer up north and winter down south? Once your goals are clear, you can start developing your cash-flow plan, which might include investments in stocks, real estate, retirement funds, or starting a business aligned with your interests.

Remember, the objective isn't just to accumulate a large sum of money. It's to build a system that continually contributes to your wealth, even when you're not actively working. By adopting this strategy, you ensure a comfortable and fulfilling retirement.

To create your retirement system:

1. Envision your retirement lifestyle and calculate the required income.
2. Explore passive income sources: investments, real estate, retirement funds, or a side business.
3. Set up efficient systems and surround yourself with competent people.
4. Balance income-generating activities with pursuits you enjoy.

EXAMPLE IN ACTION: LORI'S RETIREMENT BLUEPRINT

Lori, a high school teacher with a passion for travel and photography, embarked on her retirement planning journey with enthusiasm. She understood that relying solely on her pension wouldn't suffice to fund her dream lifestyle of exploring the world and capturing its beauty through her lens. So, she set out to build a robust retirement system.

STEP 1: ENVISIONING RETIREMENT LIFESTYLE

Lori spent evenings envisioning her retirement years. She pictured herself traversing the colorful streets of Paris, capturing the sunrise over the African savannah, and immersing herself in the tranquility of Japanese gardens. She estimated she'd need an annual income of $80,000 to fund these adventures and maintain a comfortable lifestyle.

STEP 2: EXPLORING PASSIVE INCOME SOURCES

With her retirement dreams in mind, Lori started exploring passive income sources. She decided to diversify her investments by allocating a portion of her savings to a well-balanced portfolio of stocks, bonds, and mutual funds. This would provide her with a steady stream of dividends and interest payments.

Additionally, Lori tapped into her love for real estate. She purchased a small condo in a popular tourist destination and listed it on vacation rental websites. The rental income from the property would contribute to her retirement fund while also allowing her to use the condo for her travel adventures.

STEP 3: SETTING UP EFFICIENT SYSTEMS

Knowing that managing investments and rental properties could be time-consuming, Lori set up efficient systems to streamline her finances. She automated contributions to her investment accounts and hired a property management company to handle the day-to-day operations of her rental condo. She also maxed out her contributions to her school-funded retirement accounts. These actions allowed her to focus on her teaching career and pursue her passion for photography without worrying about the administrative hassles.

STEP 4: BALANCING INCOME-GENERATING ACTIVITIES WITH ENJOYABLE PURSUITS

Despite her busy schedule, Lori made time for her hobbies. She joined photography clubs, attended workshops, and even started selling prints of her work online. These activities not only brought her joy but also generated additional income that bolstered her retirement savings.

LORI'S RETIREMENT STRATEGY

As Lori approached retirement age, her diligent planning paid off. Her investments had grown steadily over the years, providing her with a reliable source of income. The rental income from her condo supplemented her pension, allowing her to afford her travel adventures comfortably.

Lori's passion for photography flourished in retirement. She spent her days capturing breathtaking natural landscapes and vibrant cultures around the globe. The income from her photography sales added a cherry on top of her retirement fund, giving her the financial freedom to pursue her creative endeavors without constraints.

Lori's story illustrates the importance of proactive retirement planning. By envisioning her ideal lifestyle, diversifying her income sources, and leveraging efficient systems, she crafted a retirement blueprint that aligned with her passions and aspirations. Whether you're a teacher, a consultant, a speaker, or pursuing any other career, building a retirement system tailored to your dreams is key to enjoying a fulfilling and financially secure retirement.

[10]

DEMYSTIFYING TAX PLANNING

TAX PLANNING IS fundamental to managing finances, yet it's frequently overlooked. Financial success isn't just about how much you earn but also about how much of that income you retain after taxes. This principle holds true for everyone, from business owners to salaried individuals. Effective tax planning extends beyond the annual tax return. It involves continuous, informed decision-making throughout the year, influencing your tax situation. Strategic timing of significant purchases, investment decisions, retirement fund contributions, and charitable donations can all impact your tax obligations.

IMPORTANCE OF A TAX STRATEGY

Despite belief to the contrary, crafting a solid tax strategy is beneficial. It provides a comprehensive guide, illuminating your tax responsibilities while pinpointing lawful strategies to reduce them. This is not a privilege reserved for the wealthy; it's a tool for individuals at all income levels.

A strategic tax approach goes beyond mere compliance; it's about optimizing your financial scenario. Understanding the intricacies of tax laws and regulations allows you to identify opportunities for deductions, credits, and other benefits. This proactive stance on tax planning can translate into considerable monetary savings. These savings are not just figures on a balance sheet; they represent real financial resources that can be redirected towards other vital goals in your life, be it investing in education, bolstering retirement savings, or even enhancing your lifestyle.

Moreover, a well-planned tax strategy can help build long-term wealth. By minimizing tax liabilities, you effectively increase your disposable income, which can then be invested or saved for future growth. It also involves understanding how different financial decisions, from the type of investments you choose to the timing of certain transactions, can affect your tax situation.

Additionally, having a clear tax strategy can offer peace of mind. Tax laws can be daunting. A clear, well-defined strategy simplifies this process, providing a structured approach to handling your finances. It ensures that you are not only meeting your legal obligations but doing so in a way most advantageous to your financial health.

Effective tax planning is a continuous process that requires regular review and adjustments to align with changes in laws, income, and financial goals. It's an integral component of sound financial management, ensuring you keep more of your hard-earned money and use it to support your overall financial objectives.

A tax strategy is a vital aspect of financial planning that contributes significantly to your financial success and stability. By embracing and implementing a strategic tax approach, you can maximize your earnings and pave the way for a more secure and prosperous financial future.

TAXATION ON EMPLOYEES AND DIVERSIFYING INCOME SOURCES

Employees, typically known as W2 workers, often face higher tax rates. However, this shouldn't discourage employment; instead, it underscores the importance of strategic tax planning. Understanding the tax implications of your job and exploring ways to mitigate them will help you make the most of your hard-earned income. Capitalizing on deductions in health care, child care, and education credits can help you drive down your tax liability.

Relying solely on one income source, such as a salary, can limit tax-saving opportunities.

Diversifying your income through side businesses, investments, or real estate can provide additional avenues for tax efficiency. This strategy enhances your financial security and offers potential tax benefits.

USING TAX BENEFITS

Understanding and effectively using tax benefits is an important part of financial planning for both individuals and businesses. These benefits, including various deductions and credits, provide opportunities to reduce taxable income and, consequently, overall tax liabilities.

Business Expense Deductions: Businesses can take advantage of deductions for legitimate business expenses. These expenses encompass a broad range of costs incurred during a business's normal operations, such as office supplies, travel expenses, marketing, and salaries paid to employees. Businesses can significantly lower their taxable income by meticulously tracking and deducting these expenses. Accounting software makes this easier to manage, and working with an accountant, bookkeeper, or CPA (Certified Public Accountant) is helpful as well.

Tax Credits for Specific Investments: Certain investments may qualify for tax credits, which directly reduce the amount of tax owed. These credits are often available for specific types of investments, such as those in renewable energy or in certain community development projects. Unlike deductions, which lower the amount of income subject to tax, credits reduce the tax itself, making them particularly valuable.

Home Office Deductions: The home office deduction is a valuable tool for individuals who work from home. This allows a portion of home-related expenses, such as mortgage interest, utilities, and repairs, to be deducted based on the percentage of the home used for business purposes. This deduction is applicable under certain conditions and requires a clear understanding of the IRS guidelines to ensure compliance and maximize the benefit.

Properly leveraging these tax benefits requires a thorough understanding of tax laws and regulations, which can be complex and subject to change. Individuals and businesses are encouraged to stay informed about the available benefits and, where necessary, consult with tax professionals to ensure they are maximizing their tax-saving opportunities.

In practice, using these tax benefits not only reduces the immediate tax burden but also contributes to long-term financial health by preserving more income for investment, growth, or other financial priorities. It's a strategic approach that enhances overall financial planning and can lead to significant savings over time.

THE ROLE OF DEBT AND REAL ESTATE IN TAX PLANNING

In tax planning, the strategic use of debt and real estate investments can play a pivotal role. Understanding how these elements can contribute to a tax-efficient strategy is key to enhancing your financial portfolio's overall performance.

Debt, often perceived negatively, can be a boon in tax planning, especially regarding mortgages. Mortgage interest deductions stand as a prime example. Homeowners may be able to deduct the interest paid on their mortgage from their taxable income, leading to substantial tax savings. This aspect makes home ownership more attractive and turns mortgage debt into a financially strategic tool. (Note: The value of your other itemized deductions will determine whether taking the mortgage interest deduction is advantageous.)

INVESTING AS A TAX STRATEGY

Real estate investments extend the benefits further. Investment properties can offer several tax advantages, including deductions for property taxes, operating expenses, and depreciation. These deductions can significantly reduce the taxable income generated from the property, effectively lowering your overall tax liability. Moreover, when you sell a property, the capital gains tax can potentially be deferred through strategies like 1031 exchanges, providing an additional layer of tax efficiency. (The 1031 exchange lets investors swap one property for another of equal or higher value to defer paying taxes on the profit they make.)

Additionally, certain types of investment-related debts, such as loans for purchasing income-generating properties or funding business ventures, can also have favorable tax implications. The interest paid on these loans may be deductible, reducing the overall taxable income and maximizing the profitability of these investments.

The integration of debt and real estate into your tax planning strategy should be done with careful consideration and ideally under the guidance of a tax professional. These components can reduce your tax burden and contribute to building and preserving wealth. By leveraging the tax benefits associated with mortgage interest, real estate investments, and investment-related debts, you can create a more efficient and effective financial strategy, aligning your tax planning with your broader financial goals.

Incorporating debt and real estate into your tax strategy is not just about tax savings; it's about optimizing your financial portfolio for growth and stability. This approach reinforces the importance of understanding and utilizing every available financial tool to achieve a more advantageous tax position and, consequently, a more secure financial future.

PROFESSIONAL HELP IN TAX PLANNING

Given the complexity and fluid nature of tax laws, seeking professional advice is advisable. Tax advisors, accountants, and attorneys can offer tailored guidance and help you handle these complexities. Their expertise is invaluable not just for tax filing but as an integral component of your overall financial strategy. Ask your friends and colleagues for recommendations or referrals to find professionals who align with you. You can also reach out to local chambers of commerce for recommendations.

SETTING FINANCIAL GOALS

Remember those financial goals you contemplated earlier in the book? Effective tax planning is intrinsically linked to those financial objectives. Whether your goals involve saving for retirement, purchasing a home, or funding education, understanding the tax implications is important. You can achieve these goals more efficiently and with greater financial benefit through smart tax planning.

Make tax planning a proactive and integral part of your financial management, not an afterthought. By embracing a comprehensive approach that includes diversifying income sources, utilizing tax benefits, understanding the role of debt and real estate, and seeking professional guidance, you can use tax laws to your benefit. This approach optimizes your tax situation and supports your broader financial aspirations, enabling you to maximize your wealth and achieve your financial goals more effectively.

EXAMPLE IN ACTION: SIERRA'S TAX STRATEGY

Sierra is a thirty-year-old graphic designer eager to secure her financial future. She realizes that optimizing her tax strategy is necessary for achieving her goals. Sierra discovers the potential of real estate investments in reducing her tax burden and decides to explore this avenue further.

Excited by the benefits of real estate, Sierra takes action and purchases her first rental property using a mortgage. She understands that she can deduct mortgage interest from her taxable income, effectively lowering her tax liability. Sierra also plans to track and deduct eligible expenses related to property management, maximizing her tax efficiency.

As Sierra's real estate portfolio grows, she becomes intrigued by the 1031 exchange. Seeing an opportunity to defer capital gains taxes and reinvest her profits into more properties, Sierra decides to utilize this strategy. She swaps one of her investment properties for another of equal or higher value, capitalizing on the tax benefits provided by the exchange.

Recognizing that tax laws and real estate transactions can be confusing, Sierra seeks professional guidance. She consults with a tax advisor and a real estate attorney, who provide personalized advice aligned with her financial goals. With their support, Sierra addresses her issues in tax planning and real estate investment, ensuring she maximizes her tax-saving opportunities while staying compliant with regulations.

Sierra's proactive approach to tax planning and strategic real estate investments set her on a path toward long-term financial stability and wealth accumulation. Each decision she makes reduces her tax liabilities and accelerates her journey toward financial independence.

[11]

INSURANCE PLANNING

INSURANCE PLANNING is not merely about shielding yourself against unforeseen events; it's a strategy to ensure that your journey towards wealth building remains uninterrupted by unexpected setbacks. With effective insurance planning, you secure peace of mind and establish a firm foundation for financial stability.

UNDERSTANDING DIFFERENT TYPES OF INSURANCE

These days, you can get insurance for just about anything. There is rental insurance, motorcycle insurance, pet insurance, flood insurance, and so much more. Various forms of insurance can play distinct roles in your financial plan. The most common types of insurance that impact your financial position are:

Life Insurance: This type of insurance protects your family's financial stability in case of your untimely passing. It can cover expenses like medical bills, paying off debt, living expenses, and final expenses.

Health Insurance covers medical expenses, protecting your savings against health issues' potentially devastating financial impact. Long-term care insurance is increasingly important as life expectancy increases. The cost of senior care can be exorbitant.

Property (Home/Auto) Insurance: This insurance safeguards your valuable assets, such as your home or vehicle, against damage or loss. Some localities require car insurance to operate a vehicle. For renters, rental insurance is similar to homeowner's insurance. Many landlords require it as part of signing a lease agreement to protect the assets you have in your apartment.

THE ROLE OF INSURANCE IN WEALTH PRESERVATION

Insurance is useful for managing and safeguarding wealth, particularly against unforeseen events like natural disasters or accidents. It acts as a financial safety net, providing essential support in times of need. Key aspects include understanding the nuances between whole life and term insurance policies and exploring the concept of self-banking through insurance.

Whole Life vs. Term Insurance Policies

Whole Life Insurance is akin to a long-term savings mechanism. It involves paying regular premiums, and the policy provides a death benefit and accumulates cash value over time. It may also provide tax benefits for the premiums and tax-free proceeds to your beneficiaries. The cash value component offers the flexibility to borrow against it, serving as an additional financial resource. When you opt to borrow from your policy's cash value, it's important to treat it responsibly.

Term Insurance, in contrast, is more like a temporary solution. It offers protection for a specified term, such as ten or twenty years. It's typically more affordable than whole life insurance but lacks the savings element. Once the term ends, so does the coverage, and all the money you have paid in is just spent (you do not get it back). This tends to be more useful for younger families with children and a mortgage.

Self-Banking Through Insurance

This innovative approach involves using the cash value of your whole life insurance policy. You can borrow against this accumulated value, effectively granting yourself a loan. Be aware that you have to accumulate enough cash value to borrow against (which may equate to roughly 20% of the premiums paid). When there is sufficient cash value, this strategy offers the convenience of bypassing traditional banking channels and their associated constraints. But as we mentioned before, treat loans against your whole life insurance policy responsibly so it can continue to work for you. Although it's a loan against your policy, its repayment is essential for maintaining the policy's integrity and the financial benefits it provides. Plus, repayment creates a perpetual funding opportunity for you. As long as your cash value continues to grow, you will continue to have a source of funding for your private use.

SETTING CLEAR FINANCIAL GOALS

Insurance planning is not just about preparing for the worst; it's also about making strategic financial decisions. As we have said before, setting clear goals matters. With insurance, it helps in determining the right insurance coverage and how it can be effectively utilized to meet your financial objectives, whether it's retirement planning, safeguarding your family's future, or preparing for emergencies.

Insurance planning is an integral part of wealth management, not just as a protective measure but as a strategic component in wealth creation and preservation. Understanding the different types of policies and their potential for self-banking empowers you to take control of your financial future. The right insurance strategy can be a formidable ally in realizing your financial ambitions.

EXAMPLE IN ACTION: RACHEL'S STRATEGY WITH SELF-BANKING

Rachel, an entrepreneur, leveraged life insurance as a dual-purpose tool—for protection and wealth accumulation. She opted for a whole life insurance policy with a cash value component. This decision gave her financial leverage, enabling her to borrow against the policy for her business needs.

When Rachel needed funds to invest in a new business venture, she borrowed from her policy's cash value rather than pursue traditional financing. This strategy offered her more favorable terms and lower interest rates. Interestingly, the interest paid on her loan contributed back to her policy, essentially making her her own lender.

This approach allowed Rachel to support her business aspirations without derailing her other investment plans. Her business thrived, contributing to her overall wealth, while her life insurance policy continued to offer both a financial safety net and a growing asset.

Rachel's utilization of self-banking through life insurance illustrates a sophisticated approach to insurance planning, showcasing how it can extend beyond mere protection to become a key player in wealth management and growth.

[12]

ESTATE PLANNING

IMAGINE YOUR WEALTH as a treasure trove containing various valuable assets: cash, properties, and maybe a business or two. Now consider the question of what happens to this treasure when you're no longer here. Who will manage it, and how can you ensure it goes to the right people or causes? This is where estate planning comes in. It's essentially about crafting a meticulous plan for your wealth, ensuring it's managed and distributed according to your wishes.

PROTECTING YOUR ASSETS: BEYOND DIRECT OWNERSHIP

Direct ownership of your assets, while straightforward, can expose you to unnecessary risks. For example, if you personally own a property and face a lawsuit, your assets are vulnerable. However, placing your assets in structures like trusts or a Limited Liability Company (LLC) can provide a protective layer. These entities act as a shield, safeguarding your assets from personal liabilities.

THE UTILITY OF LLCS AND TRUSTS IN ESTATE PLANNING

LLCs and trusts are like specialized containers for your assets, each serving unique purposes:

LLCs: Consider LLCs as compartments within your treasure box, ideal for holding business interests or real estate. They offer the advantage of isolating liabilities. If one LLC faces a legal issue, it doesn't spill over into your other assets.

Trusts: Trusts are versatile and can be tailored with specific instructions on asset distribution. They can be set up for various purposes, like funding your children's education or supporting a philanthropic cause. Trusts ensure your assets are used exactly as you intend, even in your absence.

Sometimes, a holding company is used to oversee various LLCs and trusts. This is like having a master box that holds all your smaller, specialized boxes. It simplifies management and ensures a cohesive approach to handling your estate.

PERPETUITY OF ENTITIES IN AVOIDING PROBATE

An essential benefit of employing entities such as LLCs (Limited Liability Companies) and trusts in estate planning is their ability to bypass the often lengthy and complex probate and inheritance process. Unlike individual ownership, these entities do not cease to exist upon one's death.

LLCs and trusts offer a seamless transition of assets, ensuring that your properties or businesses are transferred to your designated beneficiaries without the typical delays and public scrutiny associated with probate. This is particularly advantageous for business continuity, as it allows operations to proceed without interruption.

In the case of trusts, assets are distributed directly to beneficiaries according to the terms you've set, which can be specifically tailored to your wishes and timelines. This direct transfer not only maintains privacy but also allows for a more efficient execution of your estate plans. However, be sure to update your trust documents every few years to address your current desires.

Similarly, an LLC can hold assets like real estate or company shares, and its ownership can be structured to pass on to your heirs, bypassing probate entirely. This ensures that your assets are managed and distributed as intended, without the potential complications and costs of probate court proceedings.

Overall, using these entities in estate planning is a strategic approach to ensure that your assets are protected and passed on smoothly and efficiently, per your wishes, and free from the burdens of probate.

ALIGNING ESTATE PLANNING WITH YOUR GOALS

Effective estate planning involves more than just safeguarding assets; it's about aligning these assets with your long-term goals. What do you wish to achieve with your wealth—do you want to support family, contribute to charities, or perpetuate a business legacy? These goals should dictate how you structure your estate plan.

EXAMPLE IN ACTION: JUSTIN'S STRATEGIC ESTATE PLANNING

Justin, a seasoned entrepreneur, approached his wealth as if it were a treasure box brimming with valuables—a nice home, a flourishing business, and various investments. With an acute understanding of the importance of estate planning, Justin was determined to protect this treasure and ensure it was used according to his specific intentions.

Justin put his home in a trust to safeguard it from potential legal issues. This strategic move ensured that his personal assets remained secure in case of a lawsuit or other legal complications, as the trust owned the property, not Justin personally. This separation provided a vital layer of protection.

Justin established an LLC (Limited Liability Company) for his thriving business. This entity functioned as a separate legal body, effectively insulating his personal assets from business-related liabilities. He also extended this strategy to his rental properties, creating individual LLCs for each. This approach allowed for the isolation of risks—if one property encountered legal or financial issues, the others and his personal assets remained unaffected.

Recognizing the need for streamlined management of these diverse assets, Justin set up a holding company. This overarching entity held his various LLCs and trusts, simplifying the administration and future handling of his estate. It served as a centralized control point, ensuring cohesive management of his assets.

Justin was meticulous in his goal-oriented trust planning. He established a trust for his children with explicit conditions. The trust was designed to release funds for specific milestones, such as their education, ensuring his children would benefit from his assets precisely as he had envisioned.

Justin's estate planning illustrates a well-rounded and strategic approach. By leveraging trusts, LLCs, and a holding company, he ensured the protection of his assets and laid out a clear path for their utilization and distribution. His plan reflected his goals and values, showcasing how estate planning can extend beyond mere asset protection to embody a thoughtful legacy.

Justin's approach to estate planning serves as an exemplary model. It highlights how effectively structured estate planning—utilizing LLCs, trusts, and a holding company—can safeguard wealth and ensure it serves the purposes you value most. Estate planning is not just about protecting assets; it's about creating a lasting legacy that reflects your goals and values.

[13]

Navigating Risk

EFFECTIVE WEALTH MANAGEMENT requires recognizing and managing risk tolerance. It's comparable to choosing the appropriate difficulty level in a video game—a decision that can define the entire experience. This process involves striking a delicate balance between your financial goals and the level of risk you are comfortable undertaking. It's about understanding how much uncertainty you can tolerate in your investments without causing undue stress or jeopardizing your financial stability. Just as gamers assess their skills and challenge themselves accordingly, investors must evaluate their risk appetite in the context of their broader financial objectives. Whether riding the highs and lows of the stock market or choosing more stable, long-term investments, aligning your risk tolerance with your financial aspirations is key to crafting a successful and sustainable wealth management strategy.

RISK TOLERANCE: FINDING YOUR COMFORT ZONE

Risk tolerance in investing is like finding your comfort spot in a swimming pool. Some investors are at ease in the deep end, embracing high-risk investments, while others prefer the security of the shallow waters, favoring low-risk options. This personal risk profile helps to shape your investment portfolio.

Understanding your risk tolerance can help you make more informed investment decisions. A high risk tolerance could lead you to invest in volatile markets or emerging business ventures, which offer the potential for substantial returns but also carry greater risk. Conversely, a low risk tolerance usually directs investors towards more stable, conservative investments like government bonds, which are known for their steady, if modest, returns.

Having clear financial goals will impact your risk appetite. If you're younger and planning for long-term goals like retirement, you might be more willing to take on riskier investments. You will have plenty of time to recover or benefit from big swings. However, for near-term objectives, such as saving for a big purchase like a house or a car soon, a more conservative investment approach is usually preferable.

MITIGATING RISK: STRIKING THE RIGHT BALANCE

Risk mitigation in wealth management is a nuanced process. It doesn't entail completely avoiding risk; rather, it's about strategically minimizing potential losses. This delicate balancing act is central to preserving and growing wealth over time.

One of the most effective tactics for risk mitigation is diversification. This strategy involves spreading your investments across various asset classes, such as stocks, bonds, real estate, high-yield savings accounts, and perhaps even commodities or alternative investments. The rationale behind diversification is simple yet powerful. When one asset class experiences a downturn, others may remain stable or even increase in value, thus reducing the overall impact of market volatility on your portfolio. It's akin to not putting all your eggs in one basket; you don't lose everything if one basket falls.

Regular portfolio reviews are another component of a sound risk mitigation strategy. The financial market is constantly changing, with various factors influencing asset performances. By periodically reviewing and adjusting your portfolio, you can ensure that your investment mix continues to align with your risk tolerance, financial goals, and market conditions. Staying informed about market trends and economic indicators also helps you make educated decisions to tweak your portfolio as necessary. Be mindful that some employees establish their 401(k) portfolios early in their working lives and need to make adjustments as time passes. Revisit your portfolio regularly to ensure it is still aligned with your goals and circumstances.

UNDERSTANDING EMOTIONAL RESPONSES TO RISK

Equally important in managing risk is understanding your emotional response to it. Everyone reacts differently to market ups and downs, and these reactions are a significant indicator of your risk tolerance. If the thought of market fluctuations and potential losses causes you considerable stress or sleepless nights, your risk tolerance is likely on the lower end. In such cases, choosing investments with lower volatility and more predictable outcomes might be more suitable.

Conversely, you may have a higher risk tolerance if you find yourself relatively unfazed by market gyrations and can maintain a level-headed approach during downturns. This disposition could make you well-suited for more aggressive investment strategies, which typically involve higher risk but also offer the potential for higher returns.

Mitigating risk is about finding the right balance between risk exposure and potential rewards, aligning with your financial goals and personal comfort with uncertainty. It requires a combination of strategic diversification, regular portfolio management, and a deep understanding of your emotional response to risk. Balancing investments and achieving long-term financial success requires a balanced approach.

EXAMPLE IN ACTION: BRIAN'S JOURNEY WITH RISK TOLERANCE

Brian is a twenty-eight-year-old engineer determined to secure his financial future. Brian understands the importance of managing risk but feels uncertain about where to start.

Brian begins exploring different investments to gauge his risk tolerance. He tries a mix of high-risk stocks and low-risk government bonds, discovering he's more comfortable with moderate risk. He enjoys the potential for growth in stocks while appreciating the stability of bonds.

Drawing from his experience, Brian decides to diversify his portfolio further. He allocates some funds to real estate investment trusts (REITs) to capitalize on long-term growth and passive income opportunities. Brian reduces risk and ensures portfolio resilience by spreading his investments across various asset classes.

Brian commits to regular portfolio reviews to stay informed about market trends and adjust his investments accordingly. He chats with his colleagues to learn what is working well for them. He monitors the performance of his stocks, bonds, and REITs, making necessary strategic adjustments. Brian understands the importance of proactively managing his investments to maximize returns while minimizing risk.

As Brian meets market volatility, he pays attention to his emotional responses. He remains relatively calm during downturns, indicating a higher risk tolerance. This self-awareness allows him to make rational decisions based on his financial goals rather than succumbing to emotional impulses.

Brian lays the foundation for long-term financial success through his proactive risk management approach. Brian builds a resilient investment strategy aligned with his financial goals and unique circumstances by exploring his risk tolerance, diversifying his portfolio, conducting regular reviews, and understanding his emotional responses.

[14]

LONG-TERM PERSPECTIVE

ADOPTING A LONG-TERM perspective is preferred in wealth creation and management. It involves focusing on how your assets can grow over years or decades rather than reacting to short-term market fluctuations. This approach requires patience, discipline, and a clear understanding of your financial goals.

IN IT FOR THE LONG RUN

Think of your financial journey like planting a tree. You wouldn't dig it up every few days to check the roots; you'd nurture it over time. Similarly, your investments need time to mature and grow. Consistent and patient investment, like regular care for a tree, is vital to seeing your wealth flourish.

Market downturns, while unsettling, are an inherent part of the investment industry. During these times, it's common to see a wave of panic selling. However, savvy investors know that staying the course is often more beneficial in the long run. Just as a tree withstands various storms to grow stronger over time, your investments, too, need to endure market volatility to achieve their full growth potential. The key is remembering your long-term financial goals during these periods of uncertainty. Panic selling can lead to realizing unnecessary losses, whereas staying invested allows you to ride out market lows and benefit from eventual recoveries.

BUYING SMART AND HOLDING ON

Smart investing involves seeking opportunities to buy reasonably priced assets, much like waiting for a discount on a favorite gadget or apparel. This approach is about recognizing value and investing consistently rather than attempting to time the market for the absolute lowest prices. Patience and research are needed here; understanding market trends and the intrinsic value of assets can guide you to make wise investment decisions. It's not just about buying low but buying smart—investing in assets that offer long-term growth potential at a price that makes sense.

Once you have invested, maintain a long-term perspective. Continuously reacting to market fluctuations by buying and selling can be counter-productive. Each transaction incurs costs and potentially disrupts the compounding growth of your investments. Instead, hold onto your investments as long as they align with your long-term objectives, whether saving for retirement, a child's education, or another significant goal. Regularly review your portfolio to ensure it aligns with these goals and adjust as needed, but avoid knee-jerk reactions to short-term market movements.

AVOIDING SHORT RUNS

The allure of making quick profits can be tempting, but it often involves high risk and can lead to significant losses. Short-term trading, or trying to profit from minor market movements, is akin to gambling and can derail your long-term investment strategy. A more prudent approach is to allow your investments to mature over time. This patience mitigates risk and capitalizes on the power of compound interest, where your earnings generate their own earnings. Over time, this can lead to substantial investment growth, far outweighing the potential gains from short-term trading strategies.

The "slow and steady wins the race" principle applies aptly to wealth management. Regular, well-thought-out investment decisions aligned with clear financial goals will likely lead to success over time. This approach involves setting specific goals and gradually working towards them, undeterred by short-term market shifts.

EXAMPLE IN ACTION: SOFIA'S JOURNEY WITH A LONG-TERM PERSPECTIVE

Sofia, a dedicated teacher, approached her financial planning with a clear, long-term vision. She started by investing a portion of her monthly salary into a diversified portfolio of stocks and bonds. Aware that market fluctuations were part of the investment journey, she focused on the potential growth of her portfolio over many years.

During a market downturn, while many around her withdrew their investments in panic, Sofia remained calm. She understood that growth requires time, much like a tree weathering storms. She held onto her investments, focusing on their long-term growth potential rather than short-term losses.

Sofia also practiced consistent investing. She utilized market dips as opportunities to buy more shares at lower prices. This strategy allowed her to accumulate assets at a reasonable cost over time, avoiding the pitfalls of trying to time the market.

Even when short-term gains were tempting, Sofia maintained her focus on her long-term objectives. Her goal was not immediate profit but rather building a substantial fund for future goals like homeownership and retirement. She periodically reviewed her portfolio, making adjustments only when aligned with her long-term financial strategy.

Over the years, Sofia's commitment to a long-term perspective in wealth management paid significant dividends. Her investments grew considerably, enabling her to purchase her dream home and build a comfortable retirement fund. Sofia's journey illustrates the power of patience, consistency, and long-term planning in achieving financial success.

Successful wealth creation and management require a balanced approach, incorporating patience, discipline, and a long-term perspective. Staying invested through market downturns, buying assets smartly, holding onto investments that align with your long-term goals, and avoiding the temptation of short-term profit chasing are all integral to this approach. By focusing on these principles, investors can find success in the market and achieve sustainable financial growth over time.

[15]

PROFESSIONAL GUIDANCE

WHEN IT COMES TO building financial wealth, it's not about going it alone. In fact, seeking guidance from a financial advisor or consultant can be wise. These professionals come in various shapes and sizes, each with their own specialties and areas of expertise. Here are a few different types and how they can help you pave your path to financial success.

TYPES OF FINANCIAL PROFESSIONALS

1. **Financial Planners:** Think of financial planners as architects for your financial future. They sit down with you, assess your current financial situation, and help you chart a course toward your long-term financial goals. They can assist in setting up budgets, planning for significant life events like buying a home or

retiring, and optimizing your investments to achieve your objectives.

2. **Investment Advisors:** If you want to grow wealth through investments, an investment advisor is your go-to person. These professionals are skilled in analyzing market trends, identifying investment opportunities, and managing your investment portfolio. They work closely with you to understand your risk tolerance, time horizon, and financial goals, ensuring that your investments align with your objectives.

3. **Wealth Managers:** These professionals take a holistic approach to managing your finances. They not only focus on investments but also consider tax planning, estate planning, and risk management. Wealth managers provide personalized advice tailored to your unique financial situation, helping you make complex financial decisions and maximize your wealth over time.

4. **Certified Financial Planners (CFPs):** CFPs are like the Swiss Army knives of financial professionals. They undergo rigorous training and adhere to strict ethical standards to provide comprehensive financial planning services. Whether you're saving for retirement, planning for your children's education, or

managing debt, a CFP can guide you every step of the way.

QUALITIES TO LOOK FOR IN FINANCIAL PROFESSIONALS

Finding the right financial professional to guide you on your wealth-building journey is essential. Here are some key qualities to look for when selecting an advisor:

1. **Expertise and Integrity:** Seek advisors who deeply understand financial markets, investment strategies, and financial planning principles. However, expertise alone is not enough; integrity is equally important. Look for advisors who are honest, transparent, and ethical in their dealings. You want someone who believes in the advice they give and always acts in your best interests.

2. **Customized Guidance:** Your financial advisor should take the time to understand your unique financial situation, goals, and aspirations. They should listen attentively to your concerns and preferences, offering personalized advice tailored to your specific needs. Avoid advisors who take a one-size-fits-all approach and instead opt for someone who is committed to helping you achieve your individual financial objectives.

3. **Proven Track Record:** When entrusting someone with your financial future, assessing their track record is essential. Look for advisors with a demonstrated history of success in financial management, both for themselves and their clients. Ask for references or testimonials from satisfied clients and inquire about their investment performance over time. A reputable advisor should be able to provide evidence of their competence and effectiveness in helping clients reach their financial goals.

By prioritizing these qualities in your search for a financial professional, you can ensure that you find a trusted advisor who will help you manage your wealth management strategy and build a secure financial future.

Now, let's talk about how these professionals can help you establish long-term financial goals, identify risk tolerance, and build a financial/investment portfolio aligned with your aspirations.

Establishing Long-Term Financial Goals: One of the first things a financial advisor will do is sit down with you to understand your goals. Whether you dream of retiring early, buying a vacation home, or sending your kids to college, they'll help you articulate these goals and develop a plan. Breaking your goals into actionable steps makes the seemingly impossible feel within reach.

Identifying Your Risk Tolerance: Investing involves some level of risk, but the key is finding the right balance between risk and reward. Your risk tolerance refers to how much volatility you're comfortable with in your investments. A financial advisor will assess your risk tolerance through discussions and questionnaires, ensuring that your investment strategy matches your comfort level. Whether you're a cautious investor or a risk-taker, they'll tailor your portfolio accordingly.

Building a Financial/Investment Portfolio: Armed with knowledge of your goals and risk tolerance, your financial advisor will construct a personalized investment portfolio designed to help you achieve your objectives. They'll diversify your investments across different asset classes, minimize costs, and rebalance your portfolio to stay on track. With their expertise, you can feel confident that your money is working hard for you.

EXAMPLE IN ACTION: TOM'S EXPERIENCE WITH A FINANCIAL PROFESSIONAL

Tom is a hardworking individual who dreams of retiring comfortably and traveling the world. However, he's not quite sure how to turn these dreams into reality, so he decides to seek the help of a financial advisor.

Tom schedules a meeting with a Certified Financial Planner (CFP) to discuss his goals and concerns. During their conversation, Tom expresses his desire to retire in twenty years and travel extensively. The CFP listens attentively and asks probing questions to understand Tom's current financial situation, risk tolerance, and investment knowledge.

After assessing Tom's situation, the CFP develops a comprehensive financial plan tailored to his needs. They recommend a diversified investment portfolio of stocks, bonds, and real estate investment trusts (REITs) to help Tom achieve his retirement goals while managing risk.

Over the years, Tom has regularly met with his CFP to review his progress and make adjustments as needed. Thanks to the guidance of his financial advisor, Tom stays on track with his savings goals, adjusts his investment strategy to market changes, and ultimately achieves his dream of retiring comfortably and exploring the world.

Seeking professional guidance from a financial advisor or consultant can be a game-changer in building financial wealth. Establishing long-term goals, identifying risk tolerance, and constructing a personalized investment portfolio can pave the way toward a brighter financial future.

[16]

REGULAR REVIEW

LIFE IS A TAPESTRY woven with changes, some joyous, like getting married or welcoming a new child, and others challenging, like facing a loss. Each of these events, whether heartwarming or heart-wrenching, profoundly impacts our day-to-day existence and financial picture. In these moments of change, the true value of an adaptable financial plan comes to light. Regularly revisiting and fine-tuning our financial plans isn't just good practice; it's essential for addressing the uncertainties of life.

THE IMPERATIVE OF REGULAR FINANCIAL PLAN REVIEWS

Life's milestones, such as marriage, parenthood, or even retirement, significantly shift our priorities and financial needs. A newly married couple might start envisioning a shared future in a new home. The arrival of a child often triggers thoughts about education funds. Each of these life events necessitates a reassessment and adjustment of your financial plan to ensure it remains aligned with your evolving goals.

Our financial circumstances can change dramatically—a promotion at work, a new business venture, or even a downturn in fortunes. Such shifts can directly impact our ability to save, invest, or spend. A robust financial plan must be flexible enough to accommodate these changes.

The global economy is constantly in flux. Inflation can affect purchasing power, or market volatility might influence investment returns. A forward-looking financial plan considers these macroeconomic factors, ensuring your financial strategy remains relevant and practical.

STRATEGIES FOR REVIEWING AND UPDATING YOUR FINANCIAL PLAN

SETTING AND REFINING GOALS

This theme runs through this book because it is important. Clarify your financial objectives. These goals could range from acquiring tangible assets like a home or car to securing intangible yet invaluable peace of mind through emergency funds. Documenting these goals gives clarity and direction, serving as guiding stars in your financial universe.

MONITORING AND EVALUATING PROGRESS

Periodic reviews of your financial performance are akin to periodic health check-ups. They assess whether you're on track with your savings targets, keep expenditures within limits, and ensure your investments yield expected returns. It's about ensuring you're staying on your charted course.

FLEXIBILITY AND ADAPTATION

Life's unpredictability necessitates flexibility in your financial plan. A sudden career change, unexpected expenses, or even a windfall—each demands a recalibration of your monetary strategy. This might mean increasing your savings contributions, reevaluating spending habits, or reallocating investment assets.

LEVERAGING EXTERNAL EXPERTISE

Winning the game of personal finance is a collaborative journey. Seeking guidance from financial advisors or even drawing insights from financially savvy acquaintances can provide fresh perspectives and informed advice. This collaborative approach can enrich your financial decision-making process.

CHARTING A RESILIENT FINANCIAL PATH

Your financial journey is unique, marked by personal triumphs and trials. It's a path that's not fixed but fluid, requiring constant vigilance and agility.

Regularly reviewing and adjusting your financial plan is more than a fiscal responsibility; it's about being proactive and prepared for life's myriad turns. It's a commitment to staying on course toward your goals, adapting to changes, and making informed choices that resonate with your life's narrative. So, take hold of your financial map with confidence, and let's march toward a future that's not just envisioned but meticulously planned and executed.

EXAMPLE IN ACTION: SAM'S FINANCIAL FLEXIBILITY

Meet Sam, a thirty-year-old copywriter with a passion for words and a knack for financial savvy. Sam had always believed in the power of planning, and there was no exception regarding finances. Starting with modest savings goals, Sam diligently crafted a financial plan that encompassed everything from emergency funds to retirement dreams.

However, life had a way of throwing curveballs, and Sam was no stranger to change. When Sam tied the knot with his long-time partner, Ashley, his financial picture shifted. Suddenly, there were shared dreams of homeownership and thoughts of future family expenses. Recognizing the need to adapt, Sam revisited his financial plan, tweaking it to accommodate their new joint aspirations.

As Sam's career flourished and promotions came knocking, their income increased significantly.

Rather than succumbing to lifestyle inflation, Sam remained grounded, channeling the surplus funds into investments and retirement accounts. Regular financial performance reviews ensured they stayed on track with their goals, avoiding unnecessary splurges and staying focused on long-term financial security.

But life wasn't always smooth sailing for Sam. Unexpected health expenses and a downturn in the freelance market posed challenges. Yet, armed with a resilient financial plan, Sam easily weathered these storms. They adjusted their budget, increased their emergency fund contributions, and sought advice from financial professionals when needed.

Sam remained committed to their financial journey, understanding that adaptability was key to success. Whether it was leveraging external expertise or refining goals based on changing circumstances, Sam embraced each twist and turn. Their financial plan wasn't just a static document but a living, breathing roadmap, guiding them through life's uncertainties with confidence and clarity.

In the end, Sam's story exemplifies the essence of financial flexibility. It's not just about setting goals but about regularly reviewing and adjusting them as life unfolds. By embracing change and staying proactive, Sam charted a resilient financial path that ensured stability and security, no matter what life threw their way.

[17]

Staying Disciplined

NAVIGATING THE WORLD of finance is much like being the captain of your own ship in the vast ocean. Just as a skilled captain remains steadfast and unmoved by the unpredictable storms or the distractions of passing ships, so must you remain focused on your financial goals. When market trends shift and economic fluctuations create waves, maintaining financial discipline is key to steering your ship safely to its destination.

Understanding Financial Discipline

Financial discipline is about making thoughtful, well-informed decisions with your money. Similar to planning a long journey—you wouldn't venture out without a detailed map and a clear route. Likewise, a solid financial plan should encompass a comprehensive understanding of your income, expenditures, and potential savings avenues. It's about charting and sticking to a course, even when temptations or challenges arise.

Imagine you're eyeing a shiny new watch in a store window. If your funds fall short, you wouldn't impulsively purchase it, right? Instead, you'd strategize—perhaps setting aside a small amount weekly until your savings suffice. This exemplifies setting a clear financial goal. Whether it's saving for a substantial investment like education or something smaller like a watch, clarity in your objectives is vital. It's about defining what you're striving for and mapping out a path to get there.

The financial world often mirrors the thrills and dips of a rollercoaster. Markets soar and plunge; trends emerge and fade. In such a fast-moving environment, it's easy to be swayed by emotions or caught up in the latest financial fads. However, the key to staying disciplined is adhering to the safety rules on a rollercoaster—remain seated and follow your plan. It's about holding steady to your financial strategy, undeterred by the market's ebbs and flows.

PRACTICAL STEPS TO MAINTAIN FINANCIAL DISCIPLINE

CRAFTING A BUDGET

Consider budgeting like setting a weekly agenda. Allocate specific amounts for various needs and stick to this plan. Budgeting helps you maintain a clear overview of your financial health. If the word "budget" makes you cringe, call it a spending plan.

CONSISTENT SAVING

View saving as a non-negotiable routine, like a daily workout for your finances. Even in small amounts, regular saving builds a sturdy foundation for future financial security. And those small amounts accumulate over time.

CONTINUOUS LEARNING AND REVIEW

As we learn from life's experiences, regularly review your financial decisions. Assess what strategies are working and which aren't, and adjust accordingly. This ongoing learning process is vital for economic growth.

SEEKING EXPERT ADVICE

There's no harm in consulting financial experts or knowledgeable friends. Expert advice can provide new insights and strengthen your financial planning, like seeking a mentor's guidance on a meaningful career goal. Learn from those who have been successful at what you are striving to achieve.

CURBING IMPULSE PURCHASES

Avoiding impulsive buying is like resisting the temptation of a quick but unhealthy snack. While it might be satisfying in the short term, it's not beneficial in the long run. (The power of impulse buys is why candy is placed next to the cash register.) Consider the long-term impact of your spending decisions on your financial health. Slipping "just a little bit" can add up over time.

CHARTING YOUR COURSE WITH CONFIDENCE

Remember, maintaining financial discipline doesn't mean you can't enjoy life. It's about making wise choices, prioritizing spending, and saving for what truly matters. By staying disciplined, you control your financial journey, directing your course toward your dreams and goals, irrespective of the tumultuous financial seas around you.

EXAMPLE IN ACTION: CONNOR'S FINANCIAL JOURNEY

Meet Connor, a thirty-two-year-old marketing executive with a passion for travel and a dream of homeownership. Despite his love for adventure, Connor understands the importance of financial discipline in achieving his long-term goals. His journey towards financial independence is marked by strategic decisions and a commitment to staying on course.

In his pursuit of financial literacy, Connor devotes time each month to reading finance-related books, seeking inspiration and guidance from seasoned experts in the field. He believes in the power of continuous learning and values the insights gained from diverse perspectives. By expanding his knowledge base, Connor equips himself with the tools necessary to succeed in the financial world.

As a professional in his prime earning years, Connor faces a myriad of temptations to spend money. From the allure of luxury vacations to the latest tech gadgets, the consumerist culture beckons at every turn. However, Connor remains steadfast in his resolve, prioritizing his long-term financial goals over fleeting indulgences. While he enjoys occasional outings with friends, Connor consciously limits extravagant expenses, opting for quality time spent together rather than costly extravaganzas.

One of the toughest challenges for Connor is resisting the pressure to keep up with his peers' spending habits. While his friends may frequent trendy clubs or embark on lavish ski trips, Connor remains grounded in his commitment to financial discipline. He recognizes that true wealth lies not in material possessions but in the freedom and security that comes from smart financial planning.

Guided by his financial roadmap, Connor seeks advice from financial planners and mentors who provide tailored strategies to help him achieve his goals. Whether optimizing his investment portfolio or fine-tuning his budgeting techniques, Connor values the expertise of those who have already been successful.

As Connor charts his course towards homeownership, he does so with confidence and determination. Through prudent saving habits, informed decision-making, and a steadfast commitment to his long-term vision, Connor steers his financial ship towards a future of stability and prosperity, empowered to shape his destiny amidst the ever-changing tides of the economy.

[18]

EMBARKING ON A LIFELONG JOURNEY

AS WE CONCLUDE our exploration of financial literacy and the essential principles of wealth creation and management, it's time to reflect on what we have covered. From shifting our financial mindset and setting SMART financial goals to the more intricate aspects of tax planning, each chapter has unveiled an aspect of financial literacy in the wealth-building puzzle. These insights and strategies form the basis for a sound financial future.

CRAFTING YOUR UNIQUE ROADMAP TO FINANCIAL SUCCESS

The path to financial success is as individual as your fingerprints, yet the principles we've discussed serve as a universal guide. They range from discerning the delicate balance between good and bad debt to embracing the lifelong learning journey and from making prudent, long-term financial choices to adopting a mindset geared towards growth and prosperity. These principles are not mere guidelines but milestones for your financial journey, irrespective of life's twists and turns.

As you forge ahead, the essence lies in personalizing these principles to fit your unique life story. Financial success doesn't adhere to a rigid formula; it's a blend of your personal ambitions, current life circumstances, and individual appetite for risk. This tailored approach ensures that your financial strategy is as unique as your life goals.

THE VIRTUE OF PATIENCE AND THE STRENGTH OF PERSISTENCE

Remember, the art of wealth creation and management is a marathon, not a sprint. It's a journey marked by patience, underpinned by unwavering discipline, and fueled by steadfast persistence. Just like a sapling gradually grows into a sturdy tree, your financial endeavors require nurturing, time, and strategic oversight to bear fruit.

THE INVALUABLE ROLE OF PROFESSIONAL GUIDANCE

Don't shy away from seeking professional advice. Financial advisors can help you achieve your financial goals, offering bespoke advice and insights tailored to your specific financial objectives and needs. Their expertise can be instrumental in helping you make choices that resonate with your long-term financial vision.

CRAFTING A LEGACY OF INFORMED DECISIONS

Ultimately, effective wealth management is about making strategic, well-informed decisions that safeguard your assets and pave the way for sustainable growth and prosperity. It's about forging a legacy that mirrors your values, ambitions, and life story.

EXAMPLE IN ACTION: JULIA'S FINANCIAL TRANSFORMATION

Take Julia's story, for instance. Julia, a dedicated nurse by profession, applied the principles outlined in this book to revolutionize her financial life. Starting with deciding what she wanted to create in her life and setting tangible goals for her savings and investments, she embraced the importance of understanding her risk tolerance. This understanding led her to diversify her investment portfolio across various assets, including stocks, bonds, and real estate, striking a balance that suited her financial aspirations.

But Julia's journey didn't stop there. She committed to ongoing financial education, staying abreast of market trends and evolving tax legislation. This knowledge empowered her to make strategic decisions, like establishing an LLC for her rental properties, which optimized asset management and liability protection. With the support of a trusted financial advisor, she crafted a comprehensive estate plan, ensuring her wealth would be managed and distributed in accordance with her wishes.

Over time, Julia's disciplined approach and long-term outlook bore fruit. Her investments matured, her assets were safeguarded, and she attained a level of financial stability that provided security and peace of mind. Her story is a testament to the transformative power of applying these key principles in wealth management, demonstrating that financial success is within reach with the right strategies and mindset.

SUGGESTED READINGS

WE'VE COMPILED a list of recommended readings and resources to enhance further your understanding of wealth creation, money mindset, financial management, budgeting, and investment strategies. These books have been selected to provide valuable insights, practical tips, and timeless principles that can guide you toward financial success. Whether you're a seasoned investor or just starting to build wealth, we encourage you to explore these resources further and apply their valuable lessons to your financial journey. Many wealthy individuals read several of these books yearly to stay mindful of their principles. (Note: Some links are affiliate links, which means we like them, and if you buy something, we may receive a small commission.)

BOOKS TO EXPLORE

Buffett, Warren. *The Essays of Warren Buffett: Lessons for Corporate America.* Cunningham, Lawrence A. (8th ed.). The Cunningham Group, 2023. https://amzn.to/4dr4b1R

Clason, George S. *The Richest Man in Babylon.* Dauphin Publications (from original 1926 ed.). https://amzn.to/3QvVwkM

Eker, T. Harv. *Secrets of the Millionaire Mind: Mastering the Inner Game of Wealth.* HarperBusiness, 2005. https://amzn.to/4dr2QYT

Hill, Napoleon. *Think and Grow Rich.* Sound Wisdom, 2019 (from original 1937 ed.) https://amzn.to/3UtXfbu

Honda, Ken. *Happy Money: The Japanese Art of Making Peace with Your Money.* Simon & Schuster, 2019. https://amzn.to/4abT2iD

Housel, Morgan. *The Psychology of Money: Timeless Lessons on Wealth, Greed, and Happiness.* Harriman House, 2020. https://amzn.to/3UwHKQ5

Kiyosaki, Robert T. *Rich Dad Poor Dad: What the Rich Teach Their Kids About Money that the Poor and Middle Class Do Not!* Plata Publishing, 2022. https://amzn.to/3JR2lK4

Robbins, Tony. *Money: Master the Game: 7 Simple Steps to Financial Freedom.* Simon & Schuster, 2014. https://amzn.to/3WwLbci

Scovel Shinn, Florence. *The Game of Life and How to Play It* (and her other complete works). e-artnow, 2019 (from original DeVorss & Company, 1925). https://amzn.to/4bmfOFe

Sethi, Ramit. *I Will Teach You to Be Rich: No Guilt. No Excuses. Just a 6-Week Program That Works* (Second Edition). Workman Publishing Company, 2019. https://amzn.to/3UvHz7N

ABOUT THE AUTHORS

MICHAEL GARRISON is a seasoned entrepreneur and business consultant with more than two decades of experience in business, real estate investment, and digital media.

As the founder of CM Complete Home Solutions, Michael has helped countless homeowners find financial relief and achieve their dreams of homeownership.

Michael is also the Executive Editor of *The Bellwether*, a leading digital lifestyle and financial magazine for entrepreneurs. With a passion for financial literacy and a knack for simplifying complex concepts, Michael's mission is to empower individuals with the knowledge they need to make informed financial decisions and to provide them with the tools to achieve financial independence and success.

Connect with Michael on LinkedIn (https://www.linkedin.com/in/michael-garrison) to learn more.

TANYA BROCKETT, MBA, is an award-winning publishing expert, producer, and strategist who skillfully guides authorpreneurs from baffled to bestseller and obscurity to influence in books and films. Over two decades, Tanya has coached hundreds of authors and entrepreneurs, trained thousands in publishing and business, and reviewed/written millions of pages of prose.

Tanya has a unique combination of business acumen and high-level publishing expertise. She has clients who have secured six-figure book deals, won literary awards, and generated seven figures by leveraging their books. Tanya has also taught book publishing and entrepreneurship at her alma mater, the University of Virginia. She has provided access to capital for thousands of businesses, garnering a nomination as a US Small Business Administration Financial Services Advocate for the Year. She has helped create hundreds of business entities and number-one best-selling authors—a winning combination of business and publishing acumen.

Tanya teaches new bestsellers through The Bestseller Worthy Formula Course. Tap into Tanya's expertise at TanyaBrockett.com and LinkedIn (https://linkedin.com/in/TanyaBrockett).

Secure business financing through Tanya's partner at https://www.7figures.app/hallageNink.

Made in the USA
Coppell, TX
04 June 2024

33097916R00079